SMALL BUSINESS MARKETING

50 EXPLOSIVE MARKETING SECRETS, IDEAS, TIPS & TRICKS TO BLOW YOUR SALES UP

2nd Edition

EHSAN ZAREI

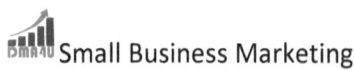 Small Business Marketing

Copyright © 2013 by Ehsan Zarei

All rights reserved. This book or any portion thereof

May not be reproduced or used in any manner whatsoever

Without the express written permission of the publisher

Except for the use of brief quotations in a book review.

ISBN: 978-1-291-72200-0

DMA4U Publishing

www.DMA4U.co.uk

 Small Business Marketing

To My Amazing Father, Wonderful Mother & Gorgeous Sisters

 Small Business Marketing

Contents

Introduction 9

#1 How small businesses can get $100 Google advertising coupon, almost free 15

#2 How to get $50 face book advertising coupon for small businesses, almost free 16

#3 What tricks can help small businesses generate more leads to their business with Google ad words 17

#4 How small businesses can use facebook advertising to find more customers 22

#5 Which online banner advertising will get small businesses to their exact target market 30

#6 How small businesses can start an affiliate program to increase their income 38

#7 Who small businesses should start an affiliate program with & why 40

#8 What tricks can help small businesses to be referred to more people 42

#9 How to post your business on 100s of free classifieds in 10 minutes 44

#10 How small businesses can find 100s of potential customers email addresses on the internet using software 45

#11 How small businesses can use SMS to find more customers 50

#12 Why small businesses should advertise on Bing search as well & why it's sometimes better than Google 55

 Small Business Marketing

#13 How To submit your website to 100s directories in less than 10 minutes & why 60

#14 Secrets of direct mail for small businesses 62

#15 Search engine optimization strategies to help small businesses get on 1st page of Google 65

#16 What Free software can help small businesses to find out what exactly your customers are interested in, it helps you make better decisions 67

#17 How Google can help small businesses find out what services or products to introduce in future based on people's search & interests 73

#18 How to register your business on Google maps, let locals find you 78

#19 What is the best way of advertising for small businesses if you want to target only 3 mile radius neighbourhood 89

#20 Where small businesses can get 5 years free website hosting 92

#21 Why & how to submit your website to top 10 search engines 93

#22 How, why & where small businesses can team up with non competing businesses for advertising 95

#23 How to a create loyalty scheme for small businesses & why 96

#24 How small businesses can use free spaces in local area to promote their business 102

 Small Business Marketing

#25 How small businesses can use their premises to advertise with a creative design which will keep you in mind of people passing by forever...106

#26 What small businesses can offer for free which will really attract customers..110

#27 How Telemarketing can help small businesses find more customers 114

#28 Why small businesses can attract more customers by providing more service than discount 116

#29 How Small businesses can be found on Google search by using social media page 117

#30 How in 24 hours you can get 1500 likes on your Facebook page, it costs $30 only 119

#31 How in 24 hours you can get 1500 followers on your Google plus page, it costs $30 only..120

#32 How in 24 hours you can get 1500 followers on your Twitter page, its costs $30 only 122

#33 How small businesses can use YouTube for FREE to generate leads to their business...123

#34 How small businesses can be found on AroundME mobile applications...126

#35 How small businesses can create offers & post them on top 10 voucher sites, its free advertising...................................133

#36 Is leaflet distribution good for small businesses ? Sometimes it's useful if you know the secrets........................135

 Small Business Marketing

#37 How charities can help small businesses find more customers 138

#38 Why small businesses should brand all their devices & how it attracts customers 140

#39 How a creative business card can make people to remember small businesses for long time, & where to get one 142

#40 How small businesses can advertise on YouTube, & why they should 145

#41 How offering a guarantee will increase small businesses sales 150

#42 How a creative unusual vehicle sign can make small businesses business popular & were to get that creative idea 152

#43 How small businesses can create real testimonials online in 24 hours & why it's important 155

#44 How & what promotional gifts will keep small businesses in customers mind for a very long time 161

#45 Where to get amazing promotional gifts for as cheap as $0.05 with free shipping worldwide 163

#46 How writing a blog can help small businesses to get found in Google 165

#47 Why small businesses should send a thank you letter & how it makes customers loyal to you 167

#48 How Google remarketing will keep showing your ad to people who visited your website once 169

 Small Business Marketing

#49 What are other low cost places on the internet for small businesses to advertise? 171

#50 Where to get 20 minutes of free marketing consultation for small businesses 176

 Small Business Marketing

Introduction

ARE YOU LOOKING FOR an easy to follow and understand marketing book specifically written for small businesses by marketing expert? A book which will teach you 50+ new tried and tested marketing techniques for small businesses.

DO YOU WANT a shortcut to save your business and yourself from wasting time and money on nonsense marketing?

YOU WILL FIND OUT answers to all these questions below, after reading this book

 Small Business Marketing

#1 How small businesses can get $100 Google advertising coupon, almost free

#2 How to get $50 face book advertising coupon for small businesses, almost free

#3 What tricks can help small businesses generate more leads to their business with Google ad words

#4 How small businesses can use facebook advertising to find more customers

#5 Which online banner advertising will get small businesses to their exact target market

#6 How small businesses can start an affiliate program to increase their income

#7 Who small businesses should start an affiliate program with & why

#8 What tricks can help small businesses to be referred to more people

#9 How to post your business on 100s of free classifieds in 10 minutes

#10 How small businesses can find 100s of potential customers email addresses on the internet using software

#11 How small businesses can use SMS to find more customers

#12 Why small businesses should advertise on Bing search as well & why it's sometimes better than Google

 Small Business Marketing

#13 How To submit your website to 100s directories in less than 10 minutes & why

#14 Secrets of direct mail for small businesses

#15 Search engine optimization strategies to help small businesses get on 1st page of Google

#16 What Free software can help small businesses to find out what exactly your customers are interested in, it helps you make better decisions

#17 How Google can help small businesses find out what services or products to introduce in future based on people's search & interests

#18 How to register your business on Google maps, let locals find you

#19 What is the best way of advertising for small businesses if you want to target only 3 mile radius neighbourhood

#20 Where small businesses can get 5 years free website hosting

#21 Why & how to submit your website to top 10 search engines

#22 How, why & where small businesses can team up with non competing businesses for advertising

#23 How to a create loyalty scheme for small businesses & why

 Small Business Marketing

#24 How small businesses can use free spaces in local area to promote their business

#25 How small businesses can use their premises to advertise with a creative design which will keep you in mind of people passing by forever

#26 What small businesses can offer for free which will really attract customers

#27 How Telemarketing can help small businesses find more customers

#28 Why small businesses can attract more customers by providing more service than discount

#29 How Small businesses can be found on Google search by using social media page

#30 How in 24 hours you can get 1500 likes on your Facebook page, it costs $30 only

#31 How in 24 hours you can get 1500 followers on your Google plus page, it costs $30 only

#32 How in 24 hours you can get 1500 followers on your Twitter page, its costs $30 only

#33 How small businesses can use YouTube for FREE to generate leads to their business

#34 How small businesses can be found on AroundME mobile applications

 Small Business Marketing

#35 How small businesses can create offers & post them on top 10 voucher sites, its free advertising

#36 Is leaflet distribution good for small businesses ? Sometimes it's useful if you know the secrets

#37 How charities can help small businesses find more customers

#38 Why small businesses should brand all their devices & how it attracts customers

#39 How a creative business card can make people to remember small businesses for long time, & where to get one

#40 How small businesses can advertise on YouTube, & why they should

#41 How offering a guarantee will increase small businesses sales

#42 How a creative unusual vehicle sign can make small businesses business popular & were to get that creative idea

#43 How small businesses can create real testimonials online in 24 hours & why it's important

#44 How & what promotional gifts will keep small businesses in customers mind for a very long time

#45 Where to get amazing promotional gifts for as cheap as $0.05 with free shipping worldwide

 Small Business Marketing

#46 How writing a blog can help small businesses to get found in Google

#47 Why small businesses should send a thank you letter & how it makes customers loyal to you

#48 How Google remarketing will keep showing your ad to people who visited your website once

#49 What are other low cost places on the internet for small businesses to advertise?

#50 Where to get 20 minutes of free marketing consultation for small businesses

With Your Passion, Intention, Attention, And Patience,

After Reading This book Your Business Will Flourish. So Turn The Page

And Begin Now

 Small Business Marketing

#1 How small businesses can get $100 Google advertising coupon, almost free

As you may already know Google advertising is one of the most effective marketing strategies, because those who search for you are ready place an order, and they are on their last step of decision making process

However Google ads can sometimes be expensive and you may not have a great return on investment

But there us is a short cut for it you can get $100 Google advertising coupons from here www.dma4u.co.uk for just $20

 Small Business Marketing

#2 How to get $50 face book advertising coupon for small businesses, almost free

Facebook advertising allows small businesses with any budget to target their ads with so many different options such as age, gender, , location, language, interests , likes and many more to help you show your ad to right people who might be interested in your products or services

However there is a short cut to pay less and its by getting a $50 facebook advertising coupon for just $19 from www.dma4u.co.uk

On next chapters you will learn how to advertise on facebook

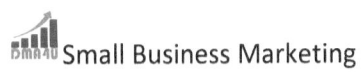

#3 What tricks can help small businesses generate more leads to their business with Google ad words

It's not easy fitting everything you want to say about your business in just a few words. Start by taking a moment to consider what you want to do with your ad. Then use the six tips in this article to create an ad that's accurate, to-the-point, and engaging – and hopefully brings you lots of clicks!

Highlight what makes your business, product, or offer unique

Free shipping? Large selection? Tell people! Highlight features or areas that make your business stand out from the competition.

Include prices, promotions, and exclusives
If you have something special to offer, make sure your customers see it. People are usually searching to make a decision about something. Give them what they need to help make their decision. For example, if you're

offering a 10% discount for a limited time, or have an exclusive product, don't forget to tell your customers!

Tell your customers what they can do

Are you selling? Tell them what they can buy. Are you offering a service? Tell them what they'll receive. Strong verbs like *Purchase*, *Call today*, *Order, Browse, Sign up, or Get a quote* tell your customers what they can expect to do when they arrive at your website.

Include at least one of your keywords in your ad text

Successful text ads tend to contain words that match a person's search. Including one of your keywords in your ad text can catch the attention of the people who searched for the **keyword**, and show that your ad is related to what they want. Additionally, the keyword you use will appear in bold in your ad, just like it does in the search results, making it more obvious how relevant your ad is. Let's say you include the keyword *digital cameras* in your ad's headline, like "Buy Digital Cameras," and a customer searches for *digital cameras*. Your

Small Business Marketing

ad's headline will appear in bold, like "Buy **Digital Cameras**." Your ad's headline could also appear in bold if a customer searched for *buy SLR cameras*, like "**Buy** Digital **Cameras**," since "buy" and "cameras" match words in the customer's search term.

Match your ad to your landing page

Take a look at the page on your website that you're linking to from your ad, which is called the *landing page*. Make sure the promotions or products in your ad are included in that page. Tell people what they can expect when they click the ad. If visitors don't find what they expect to see when they reach your site, they might leave.

Appeal to customers viewing your ad on a mobile device

When customers are on-the-go, certain information might be more useful to them (like your store location or phone number) or a particular message might grab their attention. You can show mobile customers your phone number or a map with the location of your business by using call extensions (also known as click-to-call) or <u>location extensions</u> to give customers the information they need to take action while they're on the move. Also, consider creating additional ads tailored for mobile devices, like text that highlights mobile-specific specials or discounts or a mobile-optimized display URL

Experiment

Create three to four ads per ad group, trying out different messages to see which performs the best with your customers. AdWords can automatically show the better-performing ads within an ad group more often. This removes the guesswork and lets you build on what you've learned from your experiments

For example, if the three things that make your business stand out are free shipping, seasonal discounts, and pre-order exclusives, make different ads highlighting each of those features, and see which one works better.

Tip

Capitalizing the first letter of each word in the title of your ad helps make the words stand out

 Small Business Marketing

Example

You own a camera store and want to sell your excess 8 megapixel cameras to make room for new merchandise. To find customers who are specifically searching for this camera, you decide to run a 20% off promotion. Here's what your ad could look like:

[8 Megapixel Cameras](www.example.com)

www.example.com

20% off Digital Cameras.

Free Delivery. Buy Today!

Successful text ads tend to contain words that match a person's search and tell them what they can expect when they click on the ad. Notice how the capital letters in the "8 Megapixel Cameras" ad make the words stand out

Small Business Marketing

#4 How small businesses can use facebook advertising to find more customers

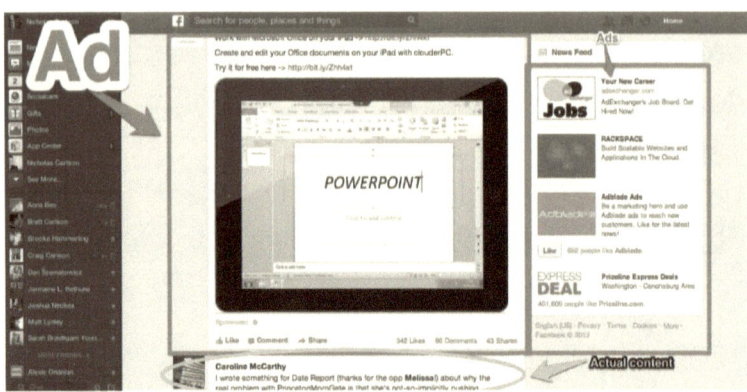

User Guide to the facebook Ads Create Tool

The ads create tool is the easiest way to create ads and sponsored stories based on your advertising objective.

 Small Business Marketing

1. Choose your advertising objective:

Go to www.facebook.com/ads/create to choose your advertising objectve and start creating your ad.

2. Create your ad:

Choose images for your ad and write the text for it. You'll be able to see a preview of your ad on the right side

Select Images for your Ad: Use up to 6 images to create more ads in your campaign at no extra cost. The more images you select, the more we can use to figure out what image is performing best and deliver that one to achieve your objective

Image recommendations for ads that appear in News Feed:

- The recommended image size is 600 pixels x 225 pixels
- The image you use for your ad may not include more than 20% text in

 Small Business Marketing

<u>the image</u> if you want it to appear in News Feed

Edit Text and Links:

Edit the text and links for your ad. You'll be able to see a preview of your ad on the right side.

The text limit for your headline and text will depend on what your advertising objective is. The character limit when you edit your text will ensure that the people you're trying to reach will be able to see your entire message.

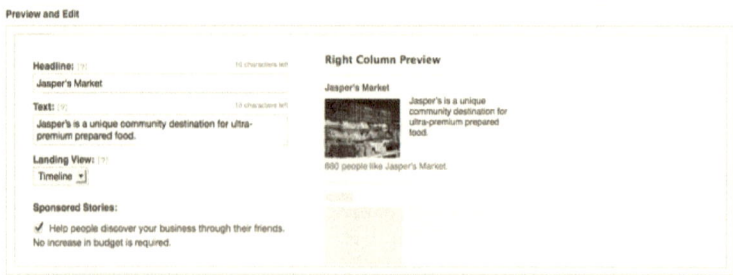

3. Choose your audience:

After creating your ad, you'll be able to identify the best audience to target

How to Choose Your Audience

Audience: There's an audience size estimation to the right indicating the total number of people in your target audience. This is the total number of people your ad will have the opportunity to reach if your bid and budget are high enough.

Location, Age and Gender: Choose the basic demographics of the audience you want to reach

Precise Interests: Choose specific interests that are important to your audience. These are determined by what people are connected to on Facebook, such as Pages and apps

Broad Categories: Select broader groups of people, based on their Activities (ex: Cooking), Family Status (ex: Parents) or Music genres (ex: Alternative). These are determined by what people are connected to on Facebook, such as Pages and apps

Connections: Select your audience based on whether or not they're connected to any of your Pages, apps or events. Anyone who has a friend connected to what you're advertising will see their friend included in your ad. This can increase the likelihood that they'll find your ad relevant enough to click or engage with it.

Keep in mind that selecting multiple options for **Connections** will limit your audience to people who only fall under each parameter. For example, if you wish to target your Fans and Friends of Fans, you will need to do so using two separate ads, one for Fans and one for Friends of Fans. Selecting both parameters for one ad will target only users who are Fans and have friends who are Fans

Advanced Targeting Options

Click **See Advanced Targeting Options** to see more ways you can target your audience.

Interested In and Relationship Status: Select the sexual preference of your audience (for people who have indicated this preference on Facebook) and the relationship status relevant for your campaign (ex: Engaged). Not everyone lists a Relationship status on

 Small Business Marketing

Facebook, so the only way to target everyone is to select **All**.

Languages: Target a specific spoken language within your target audience.

Education Select the education level or your desired audience (ex: In College).

Workplaces: Select the workplace of your desired audience (for users who have indicated this on Facebook).

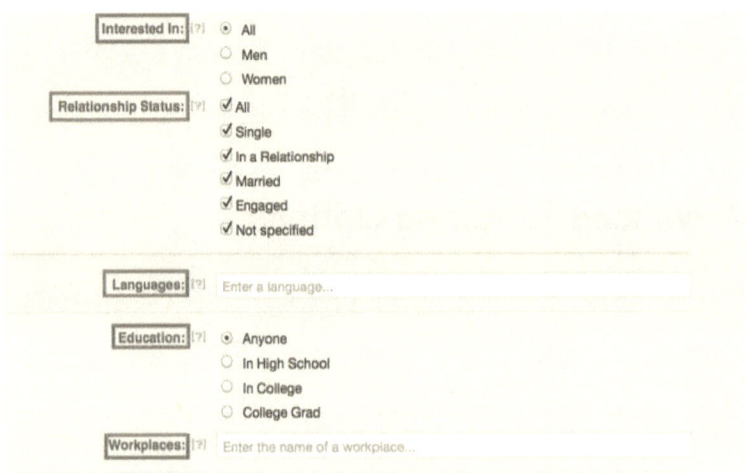

4. Choose your campaign, budget and schedule:

Name your campaign, select your budget and set the schedule for your campaign.

 Small Business Marketing

5. Set your bid and price:

Select your budget and set the schedule for your campaign. Unless you've chosen Advanced Options in the goals section, you'll pay for impressions (CPM). These impressions will be optimized so your ad shows to the people most likely to help you reach your goal. For example, if you want more people to install your app, your ad will be shown to the people who are most likely to install your app.

After you name your campaign and select your budget and schedule, place your order or review your ad so you can start reaching your audience

If you need help setting up your facebook advertising campaign DMA4U can help you visit www.dma4u.co.uk for more info

 Small Business Marketing

#5 Which online banner advertising will get small businesses to their exact target market

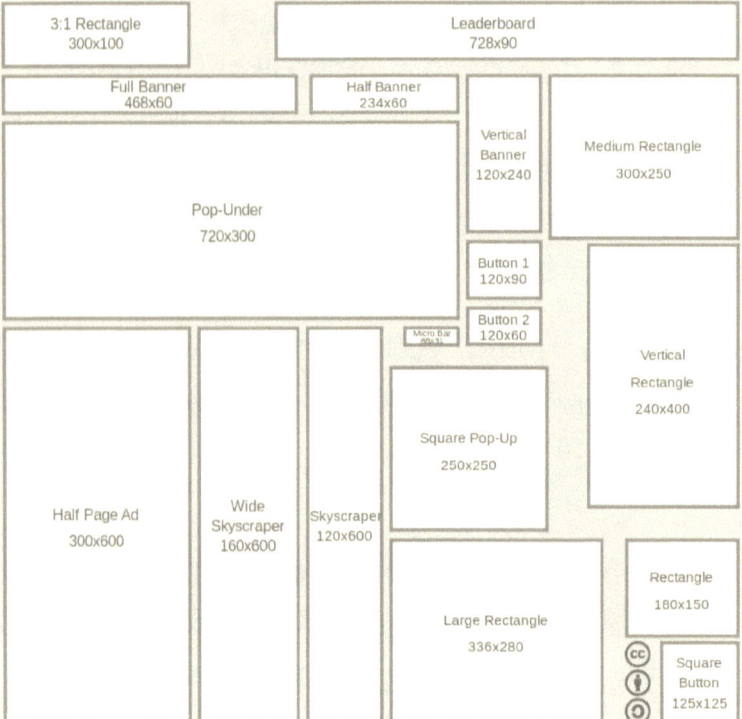

The best banner advertising to which allows you to target your exact audience is Google display advertising which allows you to advertise on all Google partners sites who allow Google ad sense,

Here more details about it are:

Overview:

Display advertising lets you

- Create all types of ads - text, image, interactive and video ads.
- Place those ads on websites that are relevant to what you're selling.
- Show those ads to the people that are likely to be most interested.
- Manage and track your budget, campaigns and results as you go

Right place, right time. That's the power of the Google Display Network

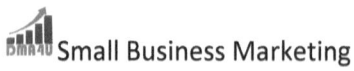 Small Business Marketing

Get inspired with different ad formats

The Google Display Network lets you place ads on a variety of news sites, blogs and other niche sites across the internet to reach more potential customer

Text Ads on websites

Image Ads on websites

Video Ads on websites

Ads on Mobile Websites

Why Display?

We're all spending more time online and 95% of that time is spent reading and engaging with content on websites. The Google Display Network can help you reach all these potential customers

Generate Awareness

The Google Display Network helps you generate awareness by getting your ads in front of consumers, so they can learn about your business as they consider their options. The more that people research in your business category, the more important it is for your products or services to stand out from the crowd.

Generate Awareness with the GDN

Build your ads

Use the **Display Ad Builder** to create high-impact image and video ads. Choose from pre-made ads or create your own ads from scratch.

Target your potential customers

Pick topics that are relevant to your business, then target sites that are related to those topics with topics targeting.

Use interest category targeting to target people who are interested in those topics, even when they're visiting unrelated sites.

Manage your campaign

With the automatic bidding tool, AdWords automatically sets the budget on your ads to maximize the number of clicks you get without paying more than you planned.

Track your investment

Once you've targeted interest categories, use Reach and Frequency reporting to measure how many people your ads are able to reach and how often your ads are viewed.

Increase Sales

The Google Display Network helps you increase sales by getting your ads on relevant sites and in front of more people, more often, so that when they come to buy, it's your business that's top-of-mind.

Increase Sales with the GDN

Build your ads

Use the Display Ad Builder to create text or image ads for free. Include offers and discounts to grab people's attention and get them to act.

Target your potential customers

Use **geographic targeting** to show the most relevant ads to people based on their

Select **keywords that are relevant to your company**, and AdWords will find websites that match your keywords.

Manage your campaign

Use conversion tracking to measure the return on investment of your ads. You decide which actions you want to track (e.g. completing a purchase) and then find out which ads bring you the most conversions and the best ROI.

Track your investment

Once conversion tracking has been set up, use the **conversion optimizer tool** to automatically manage the bids and placements for your ads. With this tool you can make sure that your ads go on the best sites that will give you the best value for money.

If you need help setting up your Google display network advertising campaign DMA4U can help you visit www.dma4u.co.uk for more info

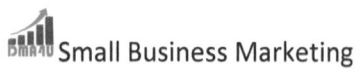
Small Business Marketing

#6 How small businesses can start an affiliate program to increase their income

Affiliate marketing is a type of performance-based marketing in which a business rewards one or more affiliates for each visitor or customer brought by the affiliate's own marketing efforts

The good thing about affiliate marketing is that you pay commission for every customer who places order for your products or services through that affiliate, so if no one placed an order you didn't lose anything,

Possibilities are endless for affiliate marketing imagine how many people or businesses you can find who might be willing to enter your affiliate program

Next chapter you will learn more on who you might be able to enter an affiliate with

 Small Business Marketing

#7 Who small businesses should start an affiliate program with & why

In all industries there are businesses that might be in same field but not competing or in other words they are not providing the same product or services as yours , and for any reason they may not be able to provide those products or services, they may lack funding , skills , etc ,

However if they had those products or services beside their own it can benefit their business and increase their income , you have to look for them and find them , offer them to join your affiliate program and in return you pay them commission for every customer they introduce or every customer who places order

To make it easier for you to convince them you should tell them how this affiliate program can also benefit their business , if beside the commission you pay them there is a benefit to their business to increase sales , you will double your chance to make them enter your affiliate program, Be creative think of giving discount to your affiliates customers, so it will encourage your affiliate to definitely introduce your products or services , because there are 2 benefits first is the commission and second he will try to increase his sales with your offer.

 Small Business Marketing

#8 What tricks can help small businesses to be referred to more people

What you may not have realized is that you can exponentially increase your sales with referrals by asking your current customers to refer you

But how to ask is important by just telling your customers please introduce me to your friends or family who might be interested in my products or services , not many people will refer even if you provided very good products or services, people are busy with their own lives and they may forget you after a while so to make them remember you should give them an offer to introduce you to others , give them an offer which will benefit them and their friends , for example if your customers friend placed an order you give both of them a discount on a product or services that might be useful to both of them

do not offer something only to your customer , the offer should be for both of them , statistics shows people may feel betraying their friends if the offer is only for them

 Small Business Marketing

#9 How to post your business on 100s of free classifieds in 10 minutes

Classifieds are amazing Free tools to promote your business in your local area, you can advertise your business in sections related to your business they have different sections such as painting and decorating, property maintenance, plumbing, heating, plastering, tiling, removal, and man y more related to all businesses

Visit www.dma4u.co.uk they can submit your business and website to 100s of classifieds

 Small Business Marketing

#10 How small businesses can find 100s of potential customers email addresses on the internet using software

Emil marketing is a free way to send your new offers to your previous customers or find new target market to email to, you probably know this but you may not know there is a software called email spider it can extract all email addresses through Google search just enter your keywords and location, it will extract all

 Small Business Marketing

email addresses related to that keyword in a few minutes.

You can get this software at www.dma4u.co.uk at half price

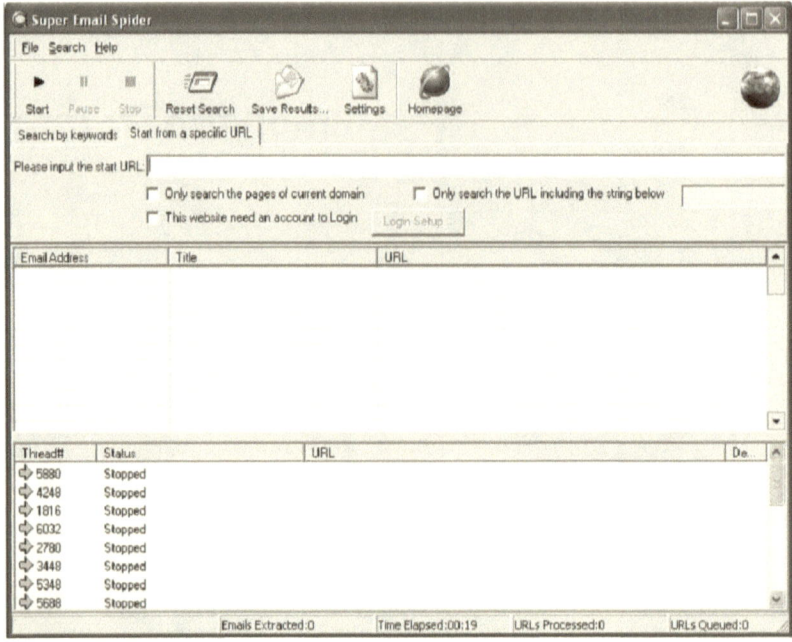

 Small Business Marketing

Here are 5 reasons why you should start email marketing

1. EMAIL MARKETING IS TARGETED Email marketing solves all the inherent problems of non-targeted marketing. Gone are the days of placing an advertisement on television, on a diner placemat, or in a periodical with no control of who will see it. With email marketing, you have the ability to control exactly who sees an email by segmenting your contacts based on their lead status, demographics, location or any other data. Targeting emails ensures that your audience receives content suited specifically to his/her needs. Email marketing makes it simple to customize your message for each customer, fostering a higher conversion rate.

2. EMAIL MARKETING INCREASES BRAND AWARENESS With each email sent, consumers are exposed to your business and your brand. With strategic planning, smart design and targeted content, your business will consistently build value. In doing so, you stay top-of-mind with your audience. Then, when a customer needs products or services, your business stands a much better chance of turning those leads into clients and clients into loyal customers.

3. EMAIL MARKETING IS EASILY SHAREABLE. There aren't many forms of marketing as easy to share as email marketing. With the simple click of the forward button, subscribers can share your deals, offers and news with their friends. Subscribers who share your emails are acting as brand advocates. Therefore, when a subscriber shares an email with friends, your brand gains more exposure and credibility.

4. EMAIL MARKETING IS MEASURABLE Analytics are indispensable to measuring the success of any campaign. Many marketing channels present ambiguous and estimated results. Email marketing, on the other hand, draws precise and valuable metrics, including delivery rates, open rates, click-to-deliver rates and subscriber retention rates. Even better: these metrics are more than just numbers and percentages. They are insights about your customers behaviors and interests. Use your email marketing campaign as a tool to monitor which information your consumers are most responsive to. From there, you can further target your marketing strategy towards more successful campaigns and topics of interest.

5. EMAIL MARKETING IS COST EFFECTIVE.

Perhaps the most appealing advantage of email marketing is the return on investment. No print costs, no postage fees, no advertising rates. Email marketing is as affordable as marketing gets. According to the Direct Marketing Association, email marketing brings in $40 for every $1 spend, outperforming search, display and social marketing.

Small Business Marketing

#11 How small businesses can use SMS to find more customers

SMS is one of the best ways to send an important marketing message, and %95 of the time people will read it, because they are not expecting an ad they will go through it find what is it all about

Visit www.dma4u.co.uk they can help you with sms marketing , with unbelievable prices , they can even find your target customers mobile numbers

 Small Business Marketing

5 Benefits of SMS Marketing

1) Instant communication

Reports suggest that text messages take seven seconds to send and deliver, on average. Plus, it's fair to say the majority of mobile or smartphone users will have their devices with them most all the time, meaning they are more likely to open the message instantly - or certainly within a short period after receiving it. In fact, IDC data shows 62 per cent of smartphone users check their phones immediately after waking up, whilst 79 per cent check theirs within 15 minutes of waking up. Few other marketing mediums can boast such immediacy, making SMS the clear winner when it comes to instant communication

2) Solid open rate

Take a second to consider this: when it comes to email, the average open rate is 27.2 per cent. Direct mail boasts a significantly higher open rate of 91 per cent Yet SMS still beats them both. The average open rate of text messages is a whopping 95 per cent making for quite an astounding difference. Whilst these other forms definitely have their place within overall marketing strategies, there's no denying that when it comes to actually guaranteeing recipients will open a piece of marketing, text messages win the battle fair and square. Plus, the higher the open rate, the greater the chances of success. It's simple!

3) Limited personal details required

With SMS marketing, those who have opted in can typically choose to hand over as much or as little information as they wish. Perhaps they just want to receive the generic discount messages, or news of upcoming sales from their favourite retailer? In this case, they can simply provide their mobile number and, at a push, their name. However others might like to receive targeted, bespoke information - like details of when their local pizzeria is offering a wine tasting evening, or fancy knowing when there are slots available at their favourite hairdresser. In this case, they can release further personal details. This flexibility should prove fairly enticing to prospects, as they are in control of the marketing, not the other way around.

4) Go green - go SMS

Want to lower your company's carbon emissions and reduce paper wastage? SMS is a medium which has a significantly lower impact on the environment than direct mail. You don't need paper, envelopes or even stamps - which means marketing costs as a whole could drop too. Statistics shows that 40 per cent of the world's trees are chopped down simply to make paper. Don't be a part of that 40 per cent - go green with text marketing.

5) Greater engagement levels

According to the Direct Marketing Association, the typical response rate on direct mail is 3.42 per cent. When you consider that the Mobile Marketing Association says people are five times more responsive to SMS marketing than direct mail, those figures add up to something pretty special. It's likely that this leap is down to the immediacy with which people can engage with a text message. Responding to a piece of direct mail usually requires completing a form, finding an envelope, addressing and stamping it, then leaving your home to find a post box. Responding to a text message takes seconds and there's no need to move from the exact spot you're in. It's so easy. Why wouldn't a company want to take advantage of that?!

 Small Business Marketing

#12 Why small businesses should advertise on Bing search as well & why it's sometimes better than Google

The main reason to advertise on bing & yahoo is its much cheaper than google, average cost per click for search advertising on bing is at least 3 timeas lower than google

Since bing & yahoo ad are not as popular as google it doesn't mean you shouldn't advertise there, because you pay per click and as long as people are looking for your services and clicking on your ad while you pay 3 times less than google search why wouldn't you give it a try and since you are a small business definitely there are enough

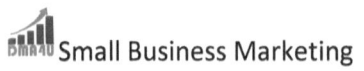 Small Business Marketing

searches on bing & yahoo search for a small a business

If you need help setting up Bing & yahoo campaign and you want to get the best result visit www.dma4u.co.uk they can help you

Here is step by step guide to quickly create a bing & yahoo campaign

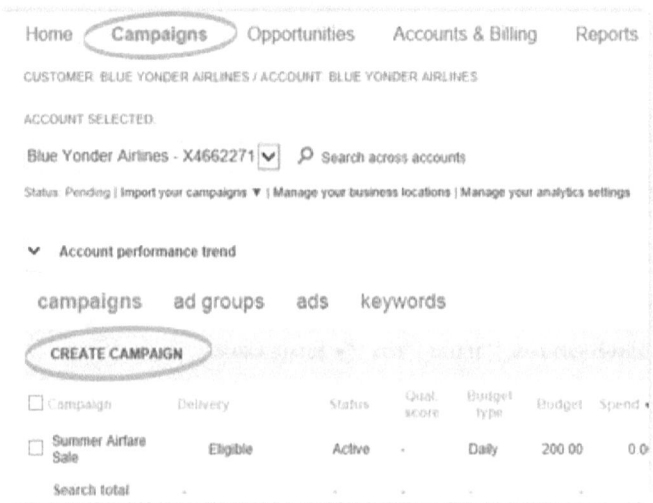

 Small Business Marketing

② Enter a Campaign name, select a Time zone, and then enter a Campaign budget.

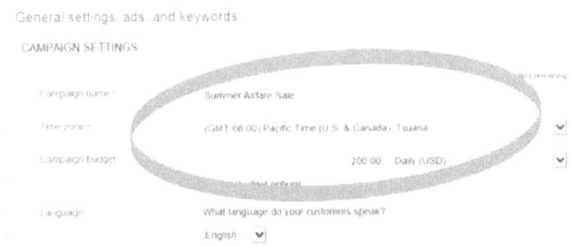

Your daily budget is the max you are charged each day.

③ Enter your Ad title, the Ad text, a Display URL, and the Destination URL.

 **Small Business Marketing**

④ Click **Research** > Select **Keyword** > Click **Add** > Click **Save**.

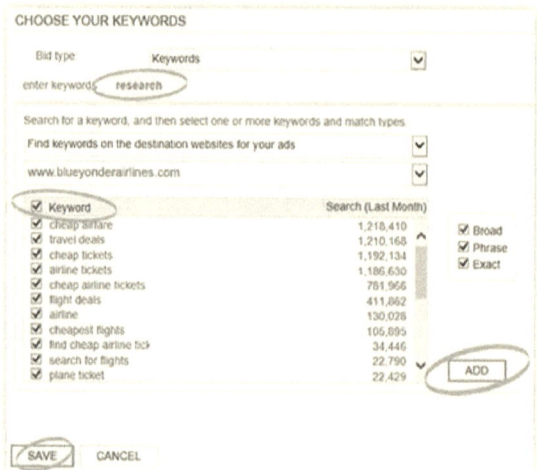

Your customers see your ads on the Yahoo Bing Network when your keywords match the customer's search query or other input. You can also type your own keywords in the box.

 Small Business Marketing

⑤ Enter a **Search network bid** and a **Content network bid** and then click **Save**.

The bids you enter in this last step are default bids that will be used if you do not enter specific bids for your keywords.

 Small Business Marketing

#13 How To submit your website to 100s directories in less than 10 minutes & why

Submitting your business details and website link on directories will have so many advantages for you it will increase your ranking in Google and other 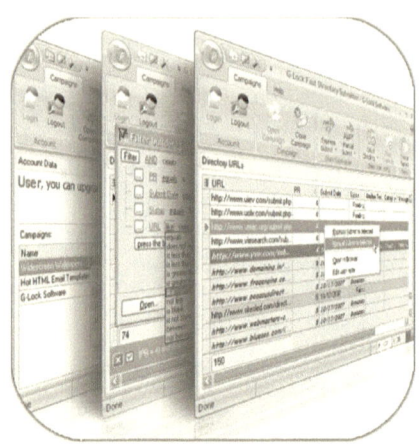 search engine , one of the most important factors in search engine optimization is directory submission the more your websites has been submitted to these directories the more your chance to be found in Google search and other search engines,

However directory submission is not only about search engine optimization and getting higher ranking in search engines, these days many people will look for your services directly through these directories, so it's really necessary to be on all these directories in your local area

If you need help submitting your website & business details to 100s of directories in 10 minutes visit www.dma4u.co.uk they can help you

 Small Business Marketing

#14 Secrets of direct mail for small businesses

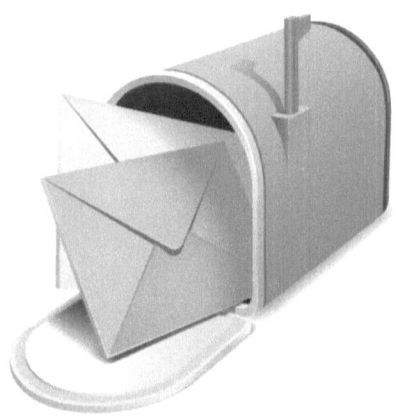

if you want a success in direct mail do not make your mails or envelope look like an ad , because if you do than more than %65 percent of your mails will be thrown away,

the secret is to look like a serious official letter so people will open it ,

Even inside the envelope you better not to put a leaflet, because again you it will be thrown away try to write something like an official letter, encourage the reader to go through the entire letter and read it all by tickling his curiosity

If you need help writing and designing an effective direct mail visit www.dma4u.co.uk for help, they have

amazing offers on how to post your direct mail at much lower price than your local post office, DMA4U can even help you find you target customers addresses in your local area

Benefits of direct mail:

- According to the United States Postal Service, 98 percent of consumers bring in their mail the day it's delivered, and 77 percent sort through it immediately. This means there are people who could be seeing your direct mail marketing campaign immediately who could potentially come looking for your business.
- Direct mail campaigns allow you to target on a specific group of individuals who are most likely to want or need the products and services your company provides. This means a higher ROI than if you were to do mass advertising, like a TV or print advertisement.
- You can customize your direct mail campaign by addressing your customers by name and addressing their needs specifically. When you speak directly to your audience, they are more likely to respond.
- There are multiple options for your direct mail campaign that can fit your direct mail

campaign needs. Choose anything from a letter to a postcard to a brochure, whichever way your message will get across the best.

- Sending a direct mail campaign allows you to physically put your message in the hands of your target audience. You can make an even greater impression by including additional material like coupons.
- Direct Mail Campaigns are easily measurable and can allow you to see exactly how effective they are for your company. Simply track the inquiries received or count the number of coupons redeemed. This will help you with future direct mail marketing campaigns by allowing you to see exactly what works for your audience.

 Small Business Marketing

#15 Search engine optimization strategies to help small businesses get on 1st page of Google

By search engine optimization you will increase your chance to be seen in Google and other search engines, Google search engine will recognise you if your business key words and links are shared on other sites, the more you share your link on other sites the higher your chance to be seen in Google search engine

You can increase your ranking in search engines by:

- Directory submissions
- Social bookmarking
- Write articles and link them to your website
- Press release submissions
- Blog posting

 Small Business Marketing

www.dma4u.co.uk provides SEO packages at very affordable prices

 Small Business Marketing

#16 What Free software can help small businesses to find out what exactly your customers are interested in, it helps you make better decisions

With Google analytics you can check what your customers are interested in when they visit your website, you find out which services they have spent time reading about, how many times they have been visiting that page, what visitors searched for you on Google to enter your website.

You can check your visitor's age, gender, geographical area and their behaviour on your website, you can even find out who referred you to your visitors

All these data will help you make decision on what products or services your customers are interested in, so you can concentrate on selling those more

You can find out what they are not really interested so you will not invest any more time or money on those products

You can find out what genders, or age is more interested on which product or service so you organize or introduce new products or services based on their preferences.

Checking geographical area will also give more details of where you visitors come from, and based their location you can find out how wealthy they are, it helps make better decision on pricing

you can check who referred these visitors to your website, let's say you have been referred by Google organic search, social medias, email or any other website, so you can concentrate in those options more to get more visitors

 Small Business Marketing

If you need help installing Google analytics on your website visit www.dma4u.co.uk they can help

Step by step guide to set up your Google analytics:

Visit www.google.com/analytics/ create an account there

Then Follow these instructions to use Google Analytics to collect data from websites.

To complete this process, you must have access to your website source code, be relatively comfortable with HTML (or have a developer that can help you), and have a Google Analytics account and property set up

To set up the web tracking code:

1. Find the tracking code snippet for your property.
*Sign in to your Analytics account, and click **Admin** in the top menu bar. From the* Account *and* Property *columns, select the*

 Small Business Marketing

property you're working with. Click **Tracking Info / Tracking Code**.

2. You should see a box with several lines of JavaScript in it. Everything in this box is your tracking code snippet. It starts with <script> and ends with </script>.

3. Copy the snippet. *Don't edit your snippet. Just copy it. You might want to paste it into a text document if you're worried about accidentally losing or changing the snippet from your clipboard.*

4. Paste your snippet (unaltered, in it's entirety) into every web page you want to track. Paste it immediately before the closing </head> tag.
If your website uses templates to generate pages, enter it just before the closing tag in the file that contains the the<head> section.

5. Check your set up. *Make sure that the tracking snippet installed on your website matches the code shown in the view,*

If it's difficult for your to do visit www.dma4u.co.uk for help

Below are some images of how Google analytics looks like

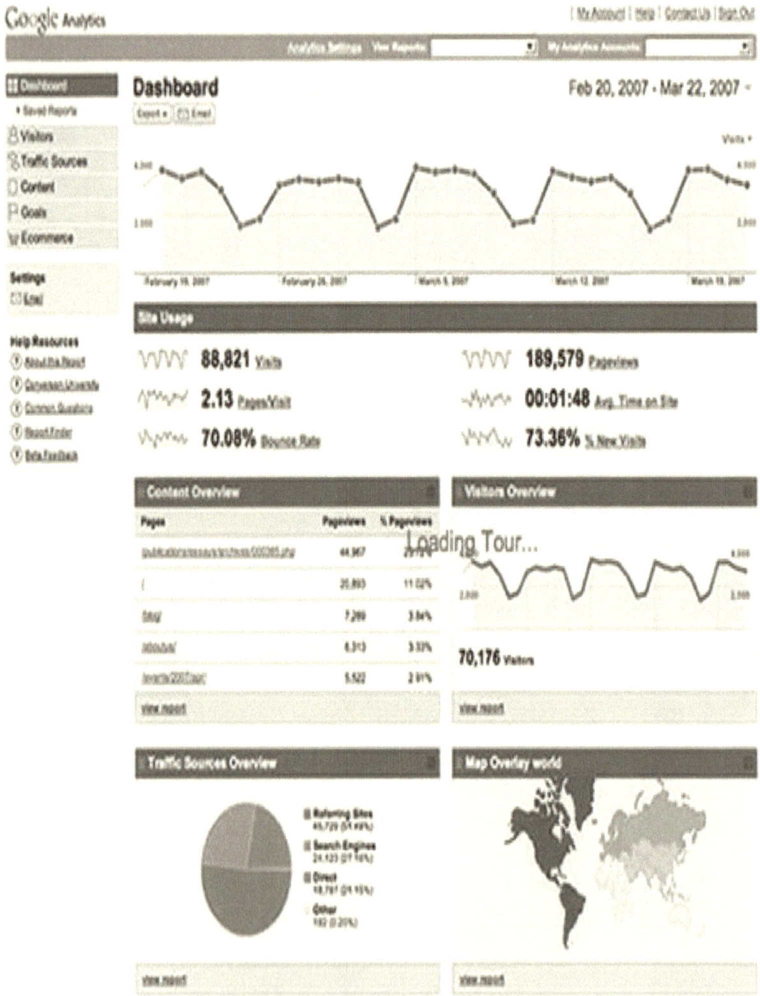

 Small Business Marketing

#17 How Google can help small businesses find out what services or products to introduce in future based on people's search & interests

Yes there is such a thing but many people do not know about, but those who know about it take a very Google advantage of it, do their market research through Google and basically they save their business on investing and spending time on something that may not really have a good result

Here is how

Visit adwords.google.com create an account there

Logging to your adwrods account,

On top menue click on Tools & analytics (see in the image here)

 Small Business Marketing

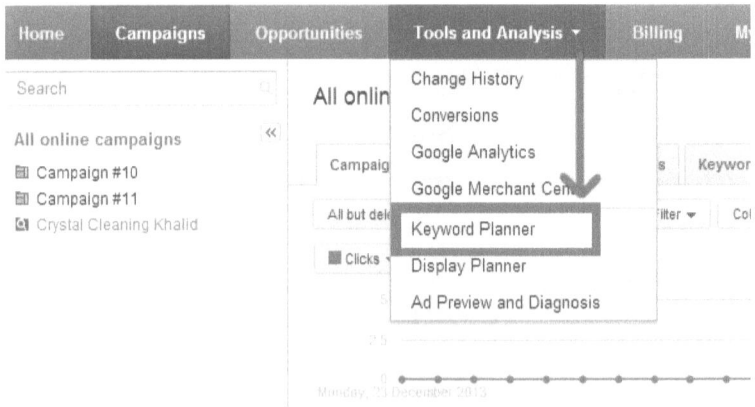

You will see this page below, then click on "search for new keyword and ad group ideas"

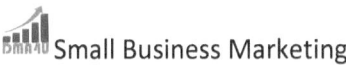 **Small Business Marketing**

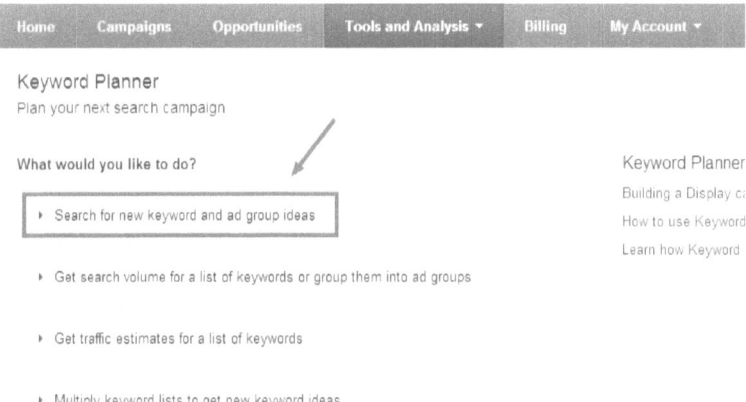

 Small Business Marketing

You will see this page

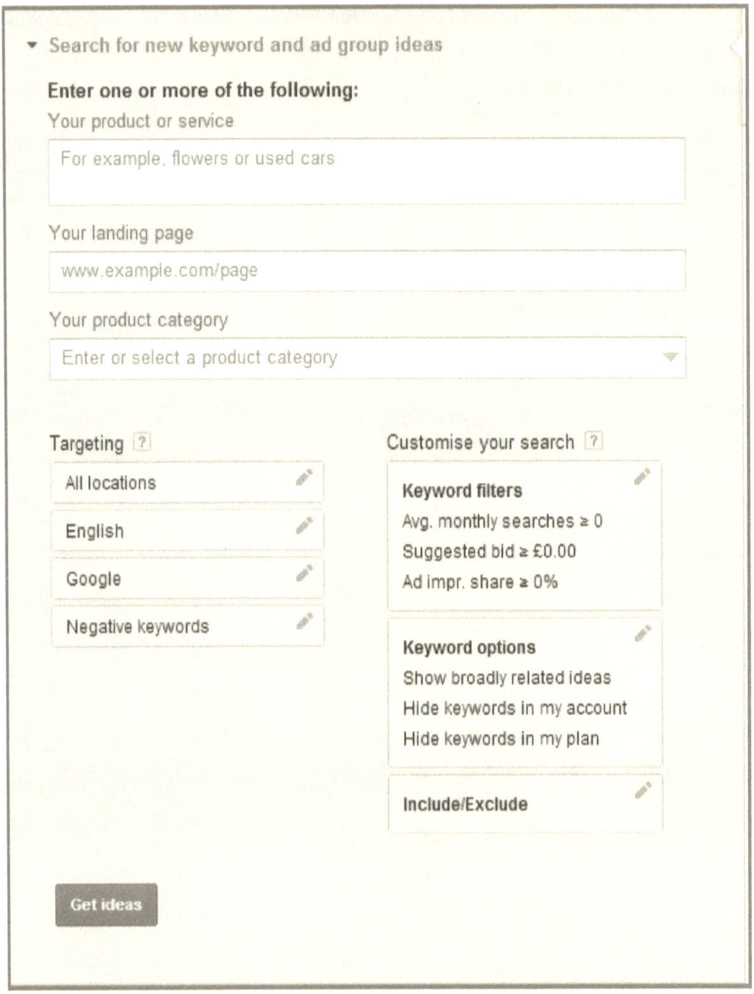

Now start your research , enter keywords you want to research about , then set location , language etc on this page , click get started you will see how many people everything are searching for that keyword ,

 Small Business Marketing

Now you should be creative and search all related keywords or phrases which is related to your business, to find is there really a demand for it before you make decision and invest in introducing a new product or services

If you need help for a professional market research for an affordable price for small businesses visit

www.dma4u.co.uk for help

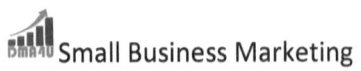 Small Business Marketing

#18 How to register your business on Google maps, let locals find you

Below are reasons why you should register on your business on google maps

Google Places for Business gives you access to free tools that help your business get online, be found on Google Search and Maps and get closer to your customers. It's the easiest way to manage your business across Google - and it's free.

Be found across Google

97% of consumers search for local businesses online. Be there when they're looking for you with a business listing – the easiest way to show up on Google Search and Maps.

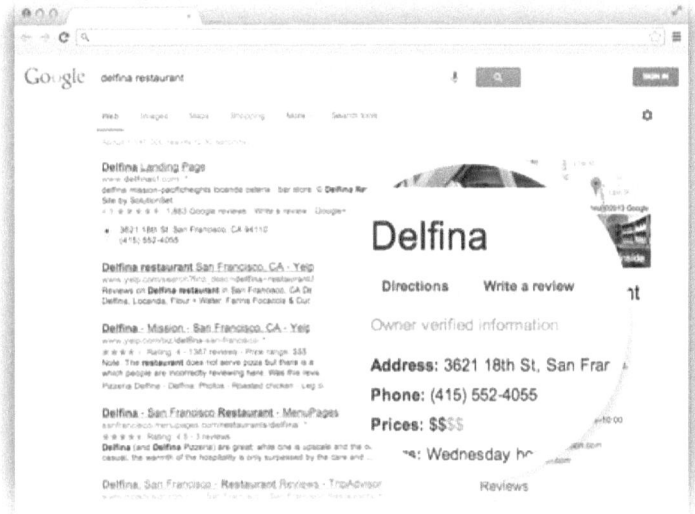

Improve your business info

Make sure that your customers find the right information about your business by updating your hours, address, contact information and photos.

Small Business Marketing

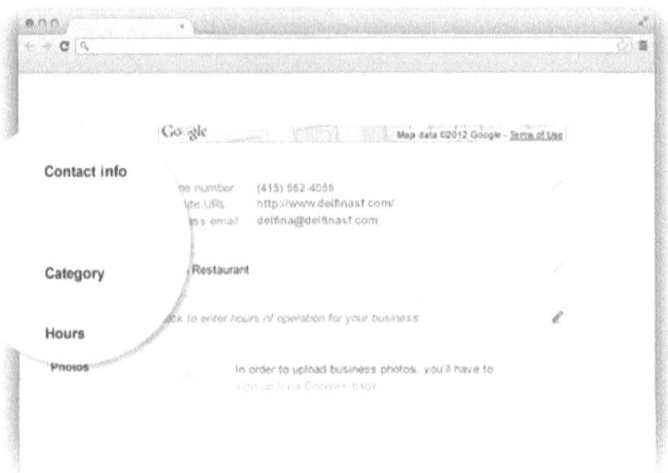

Connect with your customers

Keep your customers in the know by sharing photos, updates, news and special offers.

Small Business Marketing

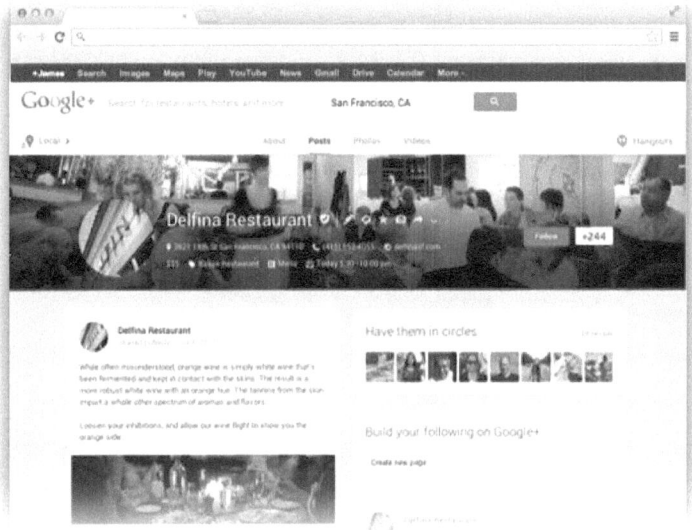

Respond to customer reviews

Understand customer feedback from across the web and easily respond to Google reviews as the business owner

 Small Business Marketing

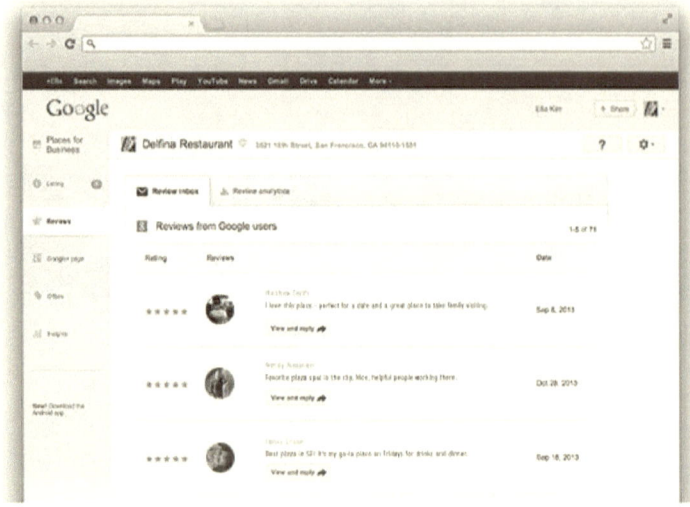

Here is step by step guide on how to register your business on Google maps:

Visit www.google.co.uk/business/placesforbusiness/

You will see this page below click on get started for free button (see image)

 Small Business Marketing

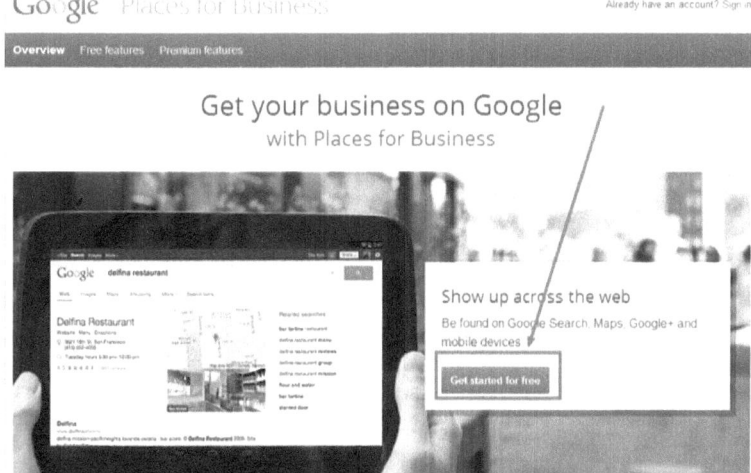

Then you will see this page below which is Google map itself

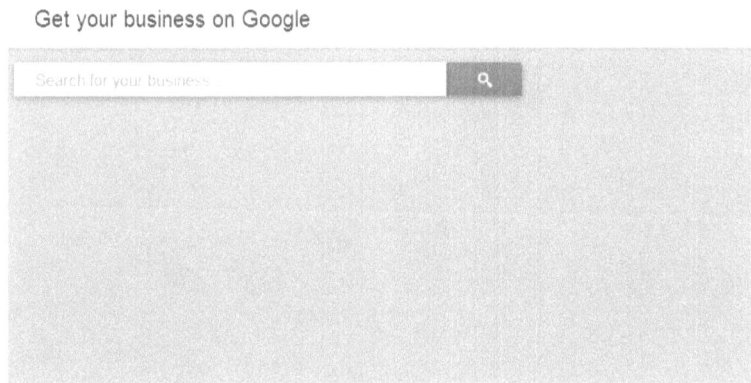

Search for you business name to find out if you are already there or not , Google

 Small Business Marketing

automatically registers many businesses there however even if you are there you should still register yourself as an admin to view and manage everything in your account,

If Google doesn't find your business you will be asked to enter your exact address and business name (see image)

Fill up the form

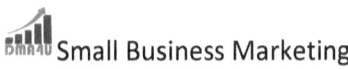 Small Business Marketing

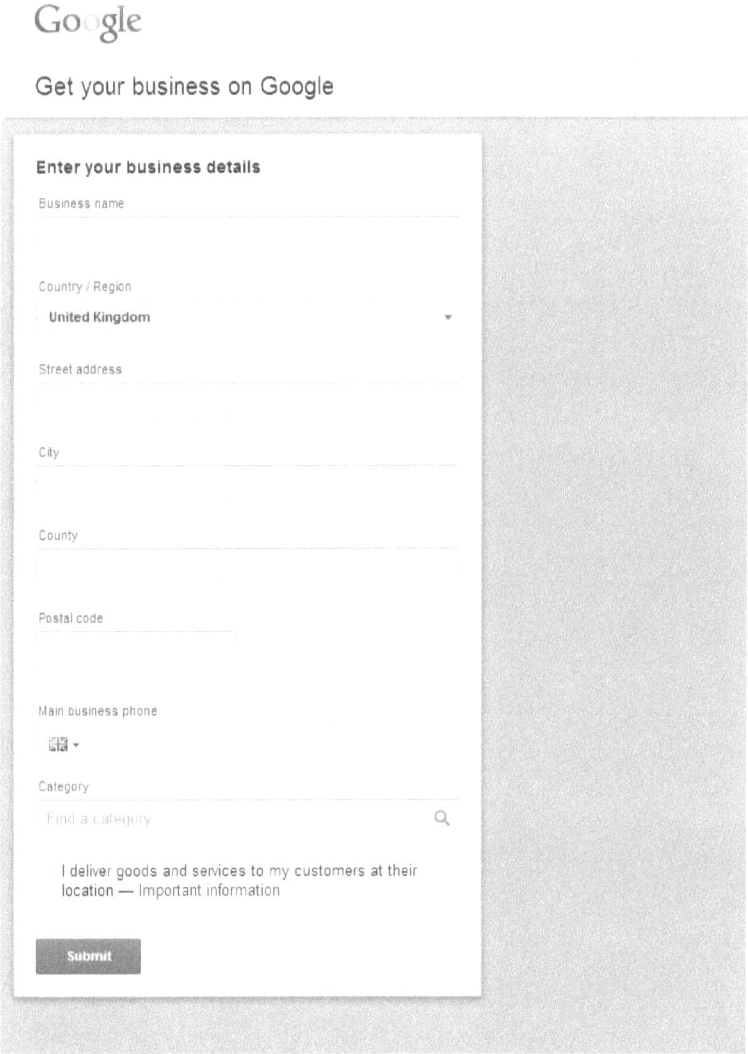

Google

Get your business on Google

Enter your business details

Business name

Country / Region

United Kingdom

Street address

City

County

Postal code

Main business phone

Category

Find a category

I deliver goods and services to my customers at their location — Important information

[Submit]

 Small Business Marketing

Then you will see this page here click on verify by post code

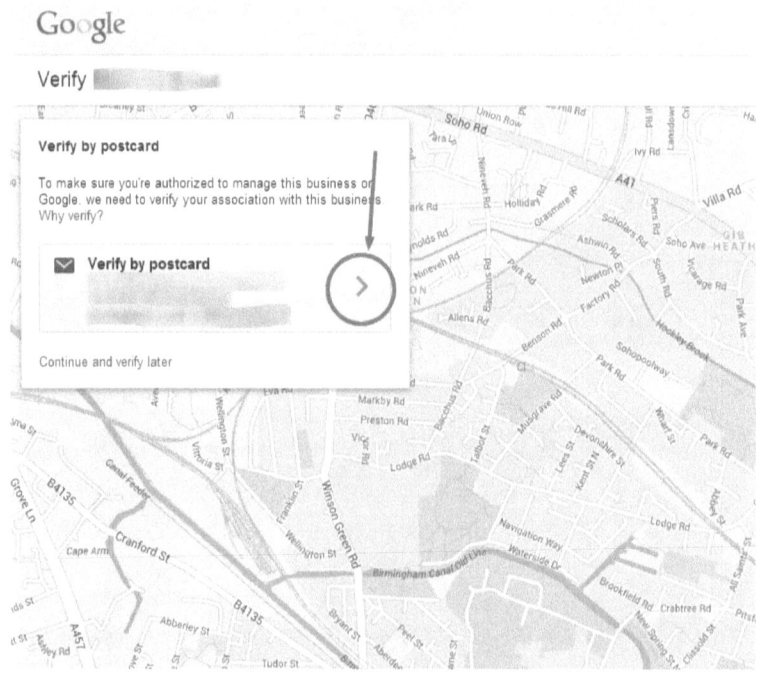

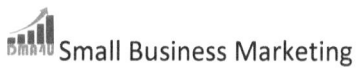 Small Business Marketing

Then you will see this page (see image)

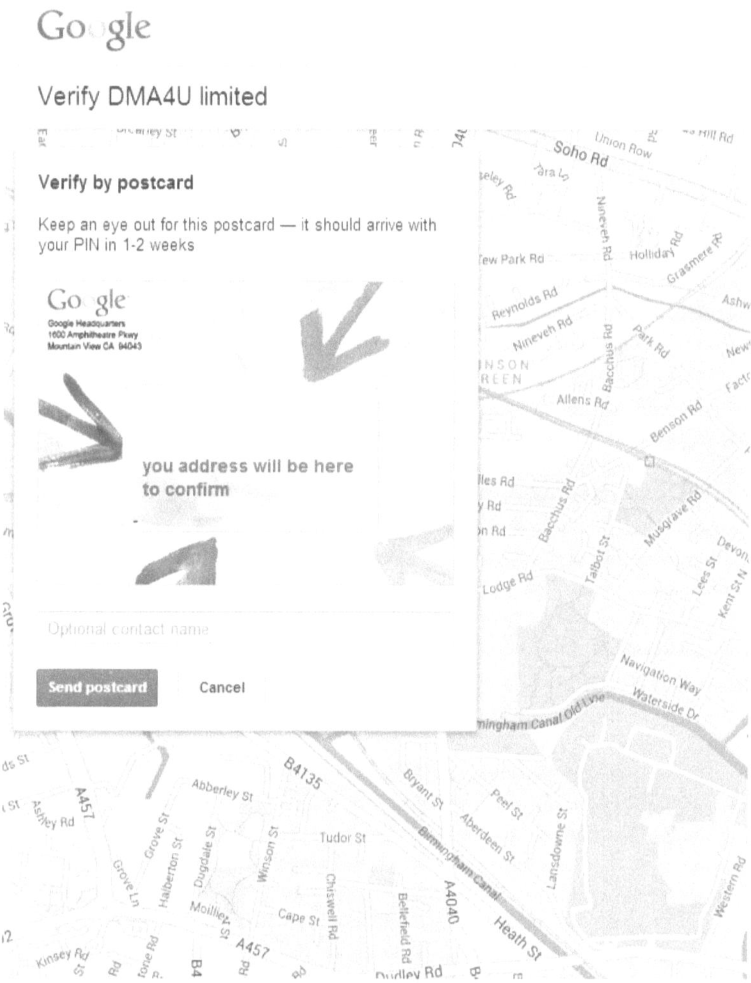

Click on send postcard and you will receive a pin code in 2 weeks time in post

Then come back to your account and enter that post code and your business will be on

 Small Business Marketing

Google maps, for those who are already on Google maps but you don't have access to manage your account , if your phone number is also available with Google they can confirm you as business owner by phone , if your number is not there , they will confirm by post

so why not to take advantage of this amazing feature and let the entire neighbourhood see you and find

if you do not have office you still can use your residential address to register your business

if you are confused or you don't have enough time to do this visit www.dma4u.co.uk they can help you

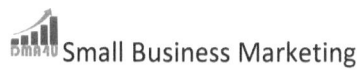 Small Business Marketing

#19 What is the best way of advertising for small businesses if you want to target only 3 mile radius neighbourhood

To stand our among your local competitors who in your local area, if someone is looking for your products or services in your area your will be the first to appear on Google maps

Here is the step by step guide to advertise with Google

However after going through this guide if you still think it's confusing or your need professional help to setup your campaign visit www.dma4u.co.uk

 Small Business Marketing

1. First register your business on google maps see previous chapter for step by step guide or visit this link

www.google.co.uk/business/placesforbusiness/

And follow instruction on screen

2. visit this page
http://www.google.co.uk/business/placesforbusiness/premium-features/

You will see this page (see image) then click get started

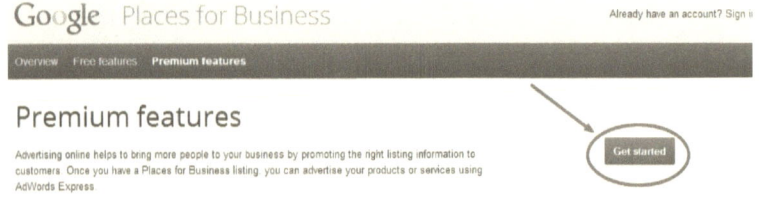

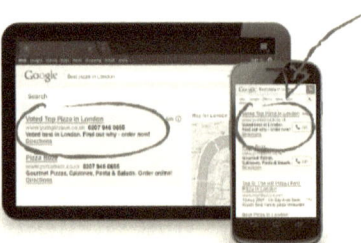

AdWords Express

AdWords Express is an easy online advertising programme, ideal for small businesses. With a click on your ad, potential customers can call you, get directions to your business or visit the business listing. That means you can reach new customers online - and get them to your door. Learn more about AdWords Express

3. If you have already been registered on Google maps you will see your business on next page choose it then follow the instruction on screen

If you need help to set up your campaign and to help you get the most out of your campaign visit www.dma4u.co.uk

 Small Business Marketing

#20 Where small businesses can get 5 years free website hosting

If you already have a website or if you don't have a website at all DMA4U can provide you with 5 years free hosting how much will that save you in 5 years ? to find out more visit www.dma4u.co.uk and ask for 5 years free hosting

 Small Business Marketing

#21 Why & how to submit your website to top 10 search engines

If you have been thinking that people only search through google are wrong there are another 9 search engines which must submit your website and business details to , if you really care about your business and want to be wherever people are looking for you, you don't have to miss any chance

These top 10 search are listed below

1) www.yahoo.com
2) www.bing.com
3) www.ask.com
4) www.search.aol.com
5) www. duckduckgo.com
6) www.home.mywebsearch.com
7) www.infospace.com

 Small Business Marketing

8) www.dogpile.com
9) www.clusty.com
10) www.google.com

to register your business on these search engines visit www.dma4u.co.uk

 Small Business Marketing

#22 How, why & where small businesses can team up with non competing businesses for advertising

Sharing your ads will save you alot of money and will benefit your business , look for non competing businesses which might be related to your business , you can find other businesses contact details on business directories , it's better for you to for businesses same size as yours , it will be easier to convince them to team up with you for advertising

you can team up for most of print advertising , such as direct mails , posters , leaflets, banner advertising, magazine advertising , etc

even for online advertising you can share each other products or services on your websites social media pages

Small Business Marketing

#23 How to a create loyalty scheme for small businesses & why

Why set up a loyalty program?

According to Jupiter Research, approximately 75 percent of consumers have at least one loyalty card. When implemented well, these programs can benefit both customers and businesses alike.

Shows customers they are valued. It is one

thing for a business to say "thank you" at the bottom of every invoice or receipt and another thing to communicate that feeling by giving a customer special offers and perks. Make people feel special for doing business with you.

Encourages return business. When people have a number of options to choose from, sometimes the mere knowledge they may earn a reward from a particular retailer is enough to influence their choice. If you place particular limits on your program - such as an expiration date - you may also be able to encourage people to shop sooner rather than later.

Helps you gather information. You can collect information from the members of your loyalty program to learn more about your customer base. For example, some programs offer you the opportuntity to track customer spending habits with your **customer management software** and gather data on demographics. Members of your loyalty program may also be more likely to return a customer survey and provide useful feedback.

Low-cost advertising. If customers see your name on a membership card whenever they open their wallet or on an email when they check their inbox, you are taking advantage of low-cost advertising. Additionally, the information gathered from these programs can help you plan out your marketing budget by identifying who is more likely to spend.

Setting up a loyalty program

Let people opt in. If you want high participation in your program, let people opt in. On your website or at your cash register, give customers the option of filling out a form to join your loyalty program, with the promise of receiving regular or occasional special offers form your business. Keep track of these email addresses

Keep it elite. If you want to limit participation to those customers who spend the most, you could consider offering invitations to a select few.

Issue membership cards or numbers.

Create a real or virtual membership card that customers can use to track their purchases and work their way up to a discount. Membership cards can be a major influence on customers' behaviour. After all, if they know it will take just three more purchases at your business to earn their reward, why would they go anywhere else?

Send regular emails. Set up an email newsletter to communicate with loyalty program members so they feel like they're part of an elite group. These emails can be filled with useful content, descriptions of new products and special offers.

For example, if you sell body care products, your email newsletter might contain tips on how to deal with dry winter skin, an explanation of the ingredients in your newest body wash and a coupon for 5 percent off of the customer's next order.

How to structure rewards?

Buy nine, get one free. This is the method used by a number of coffee shops, which give visitors their 10th drink free. You can use this as a model and tailor the specifics to your business.

Discounts. Particularly if you run a service-based business, it may make sense to offer a discount on future orders to customers who spend above a certain amount. For example, award a 10 percent-off coupon for every $100 customers spend in a single order.

Clubs. Most supermarkets offer a club-style rewards program, which tracks their purchases and permits certain advertised deals only to those who are a member. This method may work well for businesses that are keen on targeted advertising.

Rewards for paying upfront. Small business owners can offer their regular customers an incentive to pay ahead. This can also help with cash flow management.

Contests. You could hold regular contests to write reviews for products, come up with ideas for the regular email newsletter - or simply hold a raffle for all customers who spend more than a set amount in a given month.

If you need to create and design a professional loyalty scheme visit www.dma4u.co.uk they can help

 Small Business Marketing

#24 How small businesses can use free spaces in local area to promote their business

Install your banner on properties under construction or any place similar to that

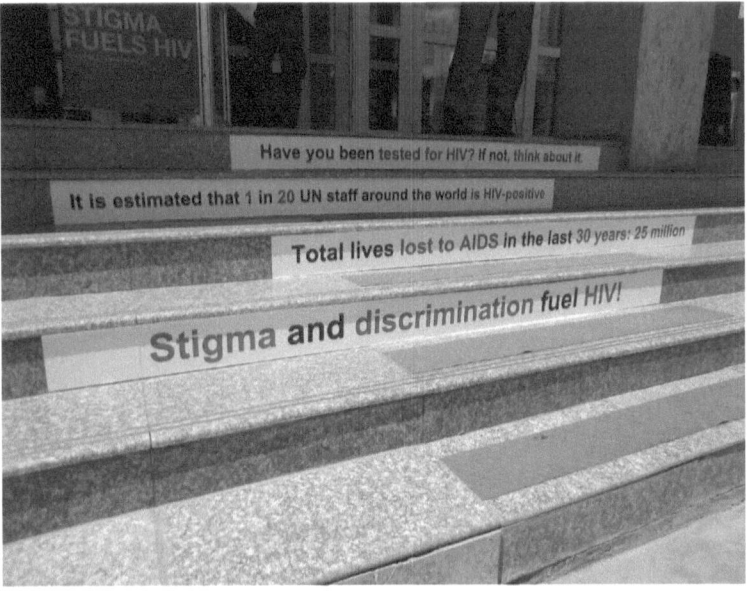

Treat your premises like a billboard, look at these images below to get some ideas:

 Small Business Marketing

Small Business Marketing

 Small Business Marketing

If you need help with a creative idea visit www.dma4u.co.uk they can help

 Small Business Marketing

#25 How small businesses can use their premises to advertise with a creative design which will keep you in mind of people passing by forever

Look at these images below to get some ideas of what you can do on your premises

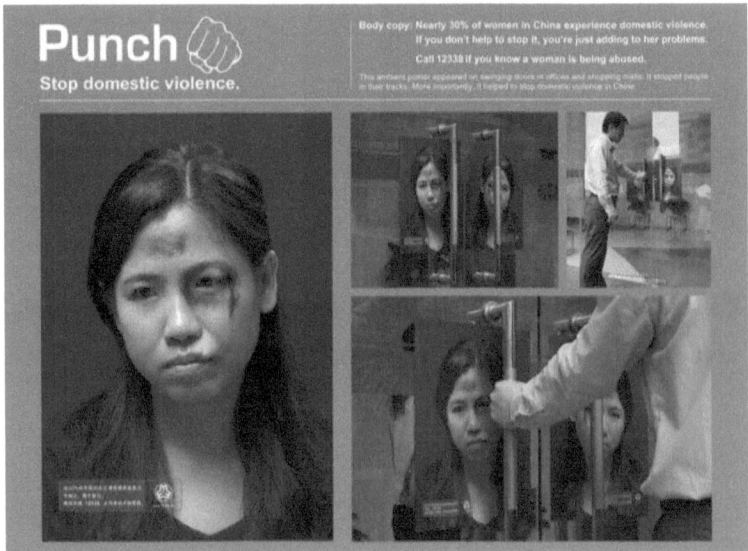

Small Business Marketing

Small Business Marketing

 Small Business Marketing

If you need help with a creative idea visit www.dma4u.co.uk they can help

 Small Business Marketing

#26 What small businesses can offer for free which will really attract customers

Here are some very effective offers

1) **Buy one get one free**: you can use these offer for low cost products, or services

2) **Gift voucher**: you can offer discount on new product or services with your voucher, the benefit is the customer will return rather than going elsewhere next time

3) **10% Off Discount**: telling your customers about a discount is a good idea if they already know your previous price, so if they see a discount they might get excited, but if you simply tell new customers who doesn't know

your product or service you won't get much out of it

4)**Student discount:** giving discount to students have a really good advantage, it spreads around very fast because most students live in shared houses or dorms, and they meet 100s of other friends in college everyday at lunch time or after classes, and if they find something exciting they tell each other

5)**Free trial:** if you have a product or services which you are able to give it for free trial you must do it , because if you have something useful and people don't still believe in it , that way they will definitely will buy it after they have tried, be creative and think it doesn't have to the entire product or service for free trial

6) **Free 'X' When You Buy 'Y'** : basically it's a trick to make people buy more, another way of giving discount if they buy 2 products at the same time, however as mentioned above talking about discount to customers who don't know about your products or services is not a

good strategy, but Free 'X' When You Buy 'Y' will work better

7) **Package Deals:** you combine a several products or services give it a lower price than buying each separately and tell the customers how much they will save if they buy it as package, they will be psychologically affected to buy if you have mixed the right products or services into one package

8) **Provide A Guarantee:** if you really trust in your own products or services give your customers a guarantee and double your sales, it gives customers a greater confidence to convince themselves to pay

9) **buy now pay later:** if you products or services worth above $99 paypal got an amazing finance for your customers, you get paid now and by paypal but your customers will have 6 months time to pay, this feature is currently only available in united states however soon it will be available in other countries for more info visit this page www.paypal.com/webapps/mpp/billmelater-productoverview

10) **free quote or consultation**: this one is a must and i guess you may already know, however i have to mention it here for those who forgot about it

If you need help creating a professional offer visit www.dma4u.co.uk

 Small Business Marketing

#27 How Telemarketing can help small businesses find more customers

Telemarketing is not only for selling a service, there are so many ways to get advantage of this low cost marketing tool, if you love your business you must all possible ways to find more customers,

Even if your products or services got no way to be sold over the phone there is still some ways to take that telemarketing can help you,

You can find other businesses contact numbers from your local business directory, invite them to your affiliate program, talk to them and try to team up with them for advertising , or at least ask them to share your products or services on their website and social medias and you do the same in return.

If you are not good at telemarketing let DMA4U help you, they can find you target wherever in the world they are contact them and introduce your offers to them , but do you what is even more amazing ? they only charge $6.6 an hour including everything, and they will even record all conversation for you, imagine in 10 hours which will only costs $66 how many people they can contact to introduce your products services etc

Visit www.dma4u.co.uk for more info

 Small Business Marketing

#28 Why small businesses can attract more customers by providing more service than discount

You don't have to always give discounts to attract customers; discounts will cut your revenue after finding a customer with so much advertisement costs and travelling costs etc.

You can offer a complimentary product or service for free

There are many examples just think about it to find out more in your trade.

This way you make your ads more attractive. Always try to be different with others even in your offers.

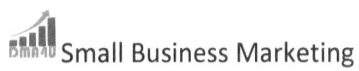 Small Business Marketing

#29 How Small businesses can be found on Google search by using social media page

Posting your website links and keywords on your social media pages is one of the most effective ways which will make search engines recognize your website as an active popular website , and as you may already know the more your website link has been shares on the internet the higher your ranking in Google search

BUT to get a much better result you must try to increase your likes and followers on your social media pages, a link of your website shared on a popular social media page with 100s of followers will give you higher credit by search engines than a social media page with no followers

Make sure you have professional cover and profile designs for your social media pages,

If you need help for professional social media pages designs visit www.dma4u.co.uk

On next chapter you will find out how to get 1000s of followers and fans on your social media pages in 24 hours

 Small Business Marketing

#30 How in 24 hours you can get 1500 likes on your Facebook page, it costs $30 only

Facebook is one the most popular social media sites and all businesses must be there, if not you are losing your customers trust, statistics shows businesses with social media pages have 80% more chance to convert visitors to customers however some businesses are shy to be on social media pages because they have no likes on their facebook pages but you DMA4U is here to help you get 1500 likes on your page in 24 hours it costs $30 only so visit www.dma4u.co.uk to find out.

by the way facebook page with more likes will increase your website's ranking on Google search

 Small Business Marketing

#31 How in 24 hours you can get 1500 followers on your Google plus page, it costs $30 only

One of the main reasons for having a Google plus page is that you shouldn't mess with king of the internet GOOGLE if they have come up with a social media site they will force everybody to sign up for it, and there are several reasons currently which are for the sake Google search engine sharing your website on Google plus will give more credit in search engines than facebook, if you want to create ad on Google ad words, there is an extension which is asking to attach your Google plus followers at the end of your ad, you are not forced to do it but if your competitors do it then you must do it too so better to act now and get yourself a Google plus and followers,

 Small Business Marketing

DMA4U can help you get 1500 followers in 24 hours for $30 only so before its too late visit www.dma4u.co.uk and get some followers on your Google plus page

As explained about facebook page , for Google plus page and any other social media pages which has more followers, search engines will give more credit to their websites which is shared on them and link to them, so if you want to be found on Google this is one the most important ways

 Small Business Marketing

#32 How in 24 hours you can get 1500 followers on your Twitter page, its costs $30 only

Twitter is another popular social media page even if you don't want to be there you have to be for the sake of search engines

To make your customers feel better about your business and trust and for your business to look professional you don't have to miss anything, you must be wherever people may have concern to see you.

You can get 1500 twitter followers if you visit www.dma4u.co.uk it costs $30 only

 Small Business Marketing

#33 How small businesses can use YouTube for FREE to generate leads to their business

Did you know YouTube is the second biggest search engine? And that not the only thing videos will appear in Google web search as well,

These days many people look for products or services on YouTube , so if you care about your business and you want to be there wherever someone is looking for your products or services you must be on YouTube too , but you might be thinking how , you might be thinking I'm not good at filming or presenting anything on a camera, don't worry there are a few tricks to get it done quickly and easily something that anybody can do,

Just take pictures of your sample products or services, and use windows movie maker to create a video out of those picture.

Windows movie maker is a software which is pre-installed on windows, just search for it in your Pc to find it, it's very simple to use just drag and drop pictures into it ,you can even drag and drop music into it and click save as movie , that's all , now you have a video

Create as many video as you can for all your services and key word upload them on YouTube and at the end of each video on description part add your website link to , attaching your website to your videos on YouTube is another way that search engines will credit your website to give you higher ranking.

Another way of using YouTube which is even much better, is to create helpful how to videos related to you business or industry you are in ,

Be creative there is always something you can say

At the end of those videos introduce your services or products

Do not underestimate the power of YouTube, you will have a lot of viewers very fast, because YouTube is not as busy as Google search you have more chance to stand out

If you need help creating 100s of videos related to your business for YouTube visit www.dma4u.co.uk they can help you do these at very affordable prices to save time

 Small Business Marketing

#34 How small businesses can be found on AroundME mobile applications

There are more than 10 mobile applications that many people these days use to find their nearest products or services,

Below are some of them , have look at these pictures to understand what they are exactly and at the end you will learn how to register on all these apps at the same time

 Small Business Marketing

Around me app

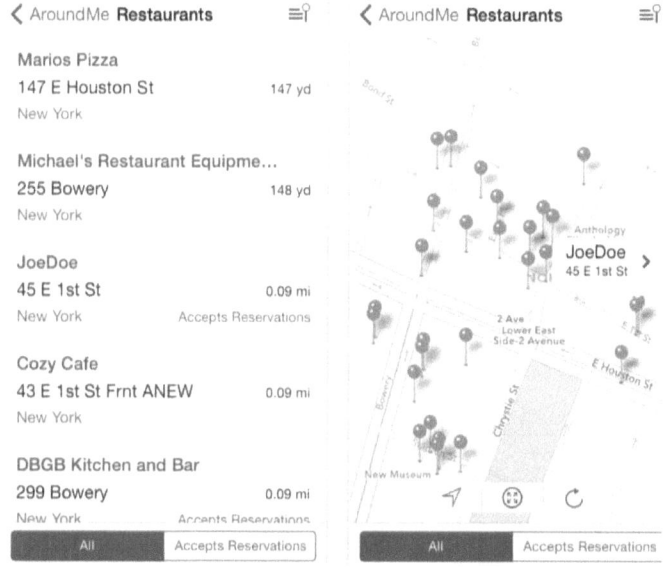

Find near me app

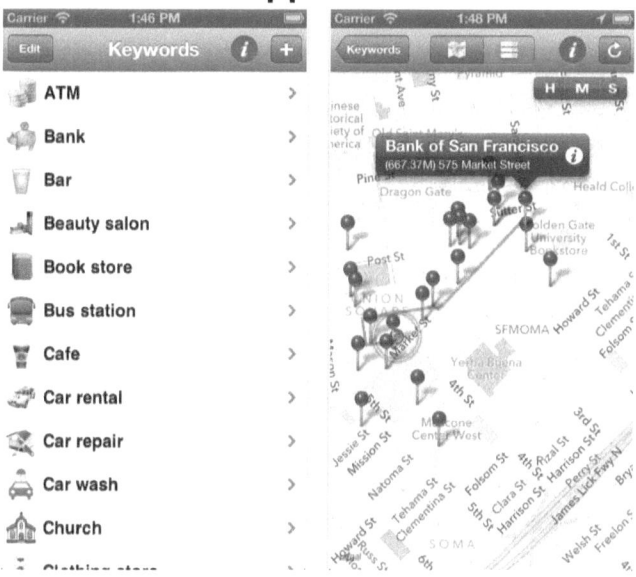

Small Business Marketing

Near me app

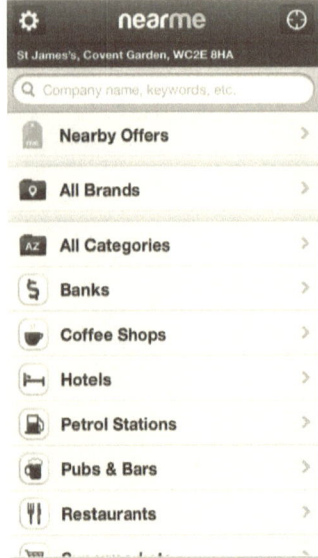

Places around

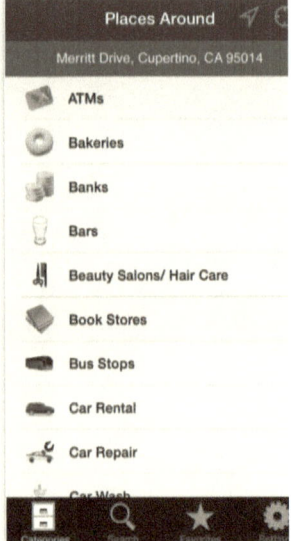

 Small Business Marketing

Wiki around me

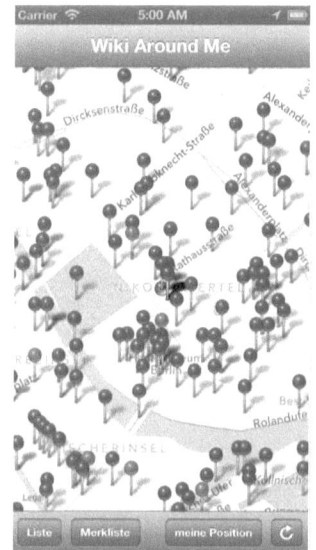 

Tagwhat, best places around app

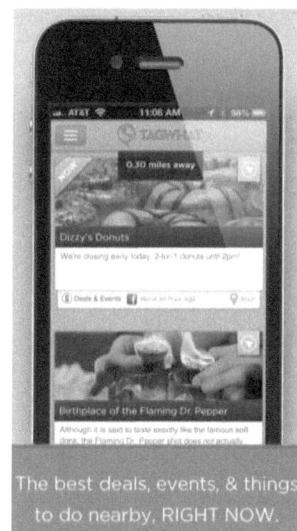 

World around me (WAM) app

Small Business Marketing

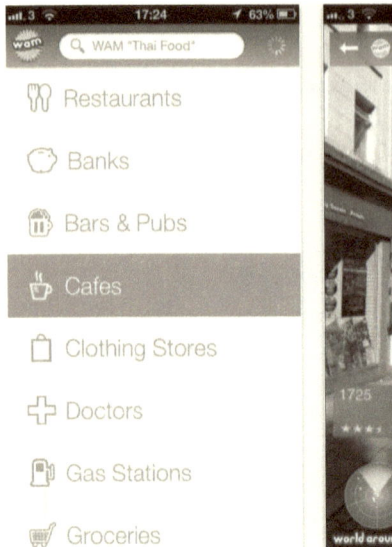

Places near & around me

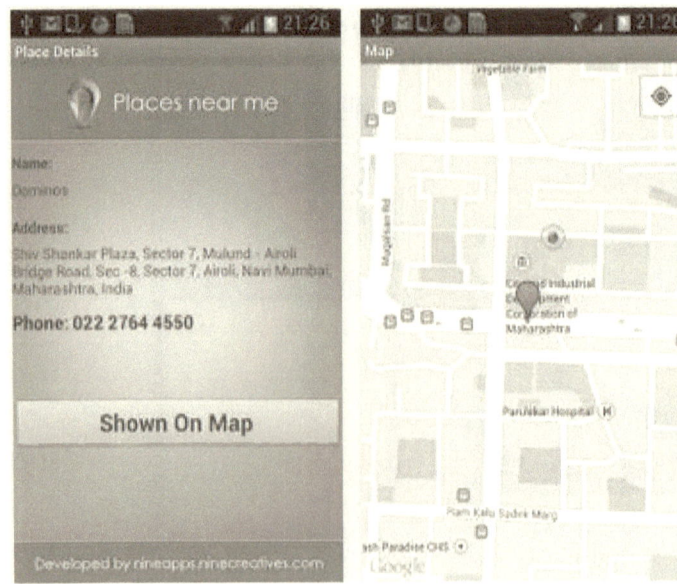

Nearby me app

Small Business Marketing

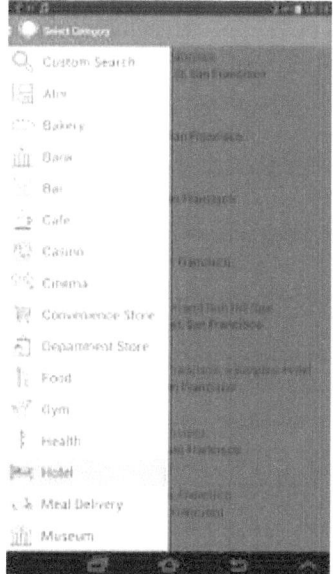 

What's around me app

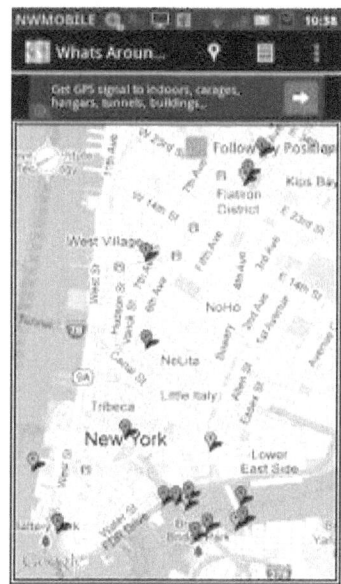 

 Small Business Marketing

You can register for all these apps at the same time by registering your business on Google Maps.

for step by step guide on how to register your business on Google maps refer to previous chapters

Small Business Marketing

#35 How small businesses can create offers & post them on top 10 voucher sites, its free advertising

Voucher websites will email your offers to all their registered member and they will also display your offer on their websites, however offer sites will charge a percentage of any offer sold through their website.

This is a free advertising for your business, they will do all the hard work to send your offer to people and you only pay them if someone placed an order,

However to stand out you and attract people you should think of a good offer to learn more about how to create a good offer refer to previous chapters

 Small Business Marketing

Below are some of these sites in the UK, to find out your local voucher and offer sites simply search for top 10 voucher sites in your country

http://www.groupon.com/

http://www.wowcher.co.uk/

www.livingsocial.com

http://www.quidco.com/

http://www.oscaruk.co.uk/

http://www.vouchercodes.co.uk/

http://www.myvouchercodes.co.uk/

http://www.hotukdeals.com/

http://www.voucherseeker.co.uk/

if you need help submitting your offer every week to 100s of voucher sites visit www.dma4u.co.uk

 Small Business Marketing

#36 Is leaflet distribution good for small businesses ? Sometimes it's useful if you know the secrets

Leaflet distribution is another marketing technique which is still alive, but you must know what to write on it, where to distribute it, how to distribute, and where to print it.

What to write on it:

As you may already know definitely there is going your contact number, products or services business name etc but these things are just so simple and will never attract a customer, you just have 3 to 5 seconds to tell

them what you have which will satisfy a need or desire.

You should make your most profitable and demanding product or service bold and add one of these to it : offer, discount, something for free or anything that can attract them to read the rest of your leaflet.

Ask your designers to use contrasting colours researches shows leaflets designed by contrasting colours will attract people to at least look at your leaflet, then as mentioned above the offer will make them read more.

How to distribute it:

One of the best ways which will save you a lot on distribution is to distribute your leaflets with non competing businesses so you can share the labour cost the best example to share your leaflets with are takeaways they are distributing leaflets everyday so simply offer them this partnership and they will be more than happy to do this with you.

Where to print and design it:

The best place to print your leaflets are online printers you can compare all prices and choose the best

However if you should try to create a unique design it will be much better since you are spending a lot on print and distribution why not to spend a little bit on a unique design so you will attract more customers and as mentioned above you just have 3 to 5 seconds to tell your customers what you can do and how you can satisfy their needs desires

If you need help for a unique leaflet or graphic design visit www.dma4u.co.uk

Small Business Marketing

#37 How charities can help small businesses find more customers

Provide some of your easy low cost services for free to charities

or give charities a special discount, this is one the best ways to advertise your business for free.

Write about this offer on your website, social network pages so many people will share it because everybody wants to help, to do something good.

You can ask local magazines, newspapers or popular websites or social networks to write about this and they would do it for free , since it's for charities,

charities in return can advertise your business, give your leaflet to their visitors talk about your business on their social media pages and website,

All these will give your business a perfect positive reputation, and those who got to know you through your help to charities will definitely keep you in mind for a long time and they will definitely refer you to others .

Below is the list of charities you can directly email them

http://www.charitychoice.co.uk/charities

 Small Business Marketing

#38 Why small businesses should brand all their devices & how it attracts customers

To make your business look professional you must attach your logo to all your devices, such as phone laptop, clothing, car, or anything else which is available in your business

It may also attract customers let's say if you have an ad on your car and you are moving around everyday imagine how many people can see it,

Since advertising is expensive why not to take advantage of things you can do for free

Even finding a few customers out of it , worth it, you don't have to miss any chance.

Small Business Marketing

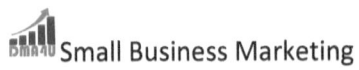 Small Business Marketing

#39 How a creative business card can make people to remember small businesses for long time, & where to get one

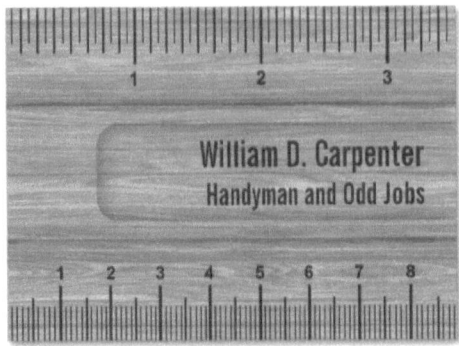

People are so busy they have so many thing in their wallet and so many printed ads around their home and business so they are not really going to keep yur business card unless its something unique and creative,

To make your business card unique you need a unique design which can be done an affordable price www.dma4u.co.uk

The paper quality of your business card is also very important which will have to ask your graphic designer or print company to show samples

Small Business Marketing

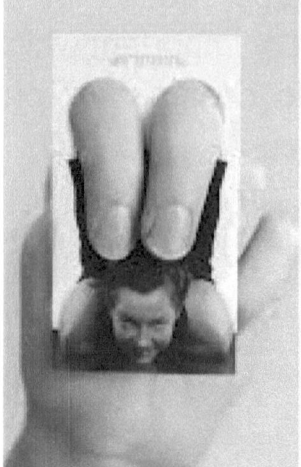

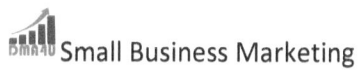 Small Business Marketing

#40 How small businesses can advertise on YouTube, & why they should

You can advertise on YouTube as well , you can target your ad to appear on videos with subjects related to what you want to advertise , so it can get to an exact target market,

Sometimes there might be some products or services which will attract your customers by seeing in action, and that's when advertising on YouTube is a must

Sometimes videos are more powerful for some products or services and will have a better impact of convincing your target market

 Small Business Marketing

How to advertise on YouTube:

Before videos

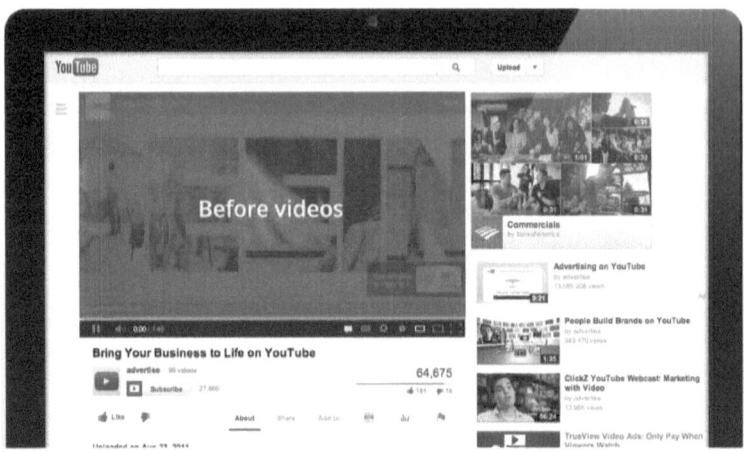

Beside videos

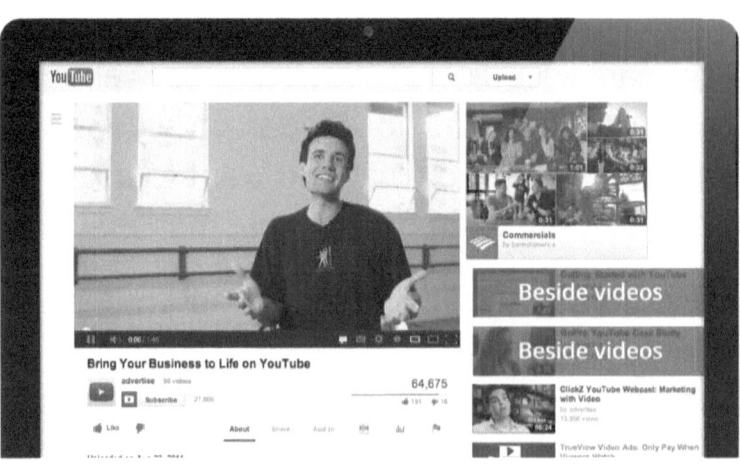

In search results

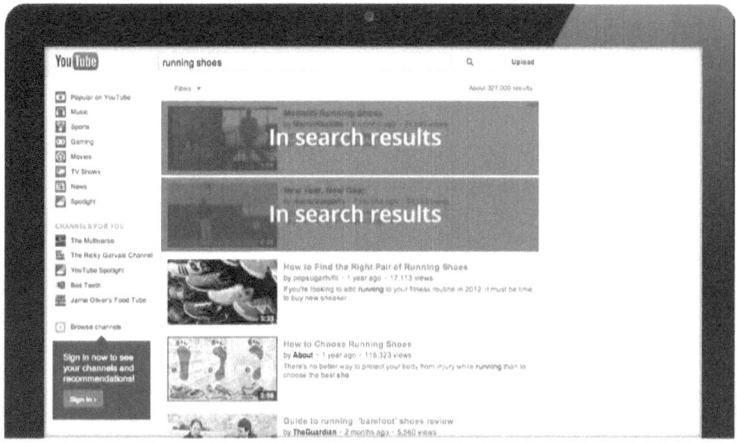

Reasons why YouTube ads work

Only pay when people watch

With video ads you pay only when someone chooses to watch your ad, so you don't waste money advertising to people who aren't interested in your business.

 Small Business Marketing

Reach your ideal customer

Zero in on the right people based on who they are, where they're located and what they're interested in – for example, men aged 18-34 in Birmingham or women who enjoy travelling.

Show up across devices

Your customers are on the go. Whether they're on a smartphone, tablet or computer your video ads can reach them. 25% of all

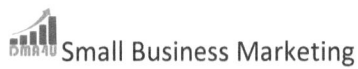 Small Business Marketing

YouTube views originate from a mobile device.

See what's working

YouTube's free Analytics tool helps you understand who's watching your ads and how they're interacting with them.

 Small Business Marketing

#41 How offering a guarantee will increase small businesses sales

When people are making decision to pay for a product or service there will be a lot of things in going on their mind , they will ask themselves many questions and they try to convince themselves how this product or service can fulfil all my needs or desires, their mind will get very busy with all these thoughts while thinking about their budget and getting a good deal , they don't have to only convince themselves they will have to convince family and friends about their decision too , it's not because someone else is going to pay for it , they want to feel good when others ask them about the product or service they paid for.

So if you have a good price, good product or service and you trust it yourself , but your customers may still have some doubts about it or maybe the customer is confused to make a decision because of too many thoughts in his mind, you can close that sale by offering a guarantee, it gives your confused customer a confidence to act now

You may have experienced losing customers who contacted you or visited you, they were willing to buy but at the end they didn't, if you don't want to those customers who come to you after all those hard work you put into marketing to bring them in to visit or contact you , then offer them a guarantee , Give them that confidence to place order , it will double your sales .

 Small Business Marketing

#42 How a creative unusual vehicle sign can make small businesses business popular & were to get that creative idea

Put your car to work for you as an advertising agent, it goes around every day, imagine how many people will see your car a year.

But imagine if there some unique unusual ad on your car, all those people will remember your car and best of all they remember your product or service you are offering as well,

 Small Business Marketing

But do you what's even more special that many people will take pictures and videos upload them on social media pages, and show their friends,

It will be a free unlimited marketing for your business,

To get a unique design for your vehicle visit www.dma4u.co.uk

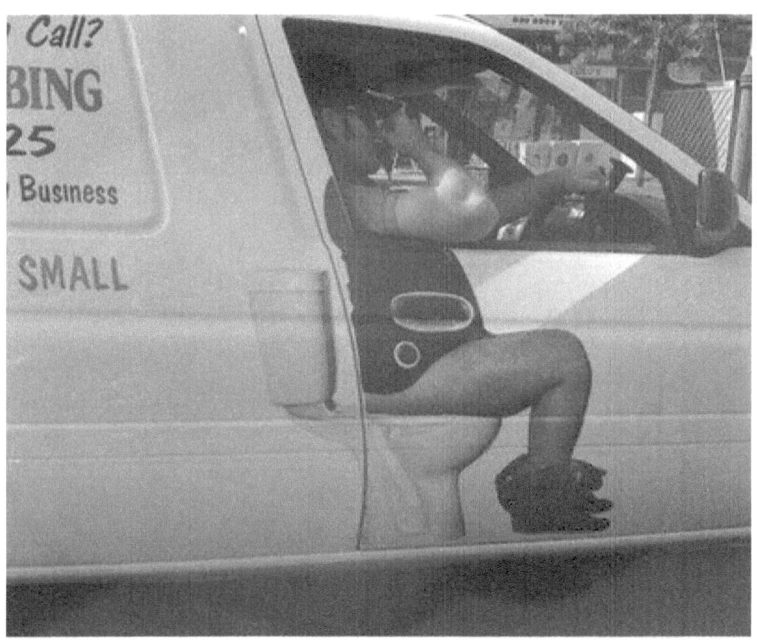

Small Business Marketing

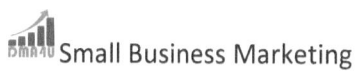 Small Business Marketing

#43 How small businesses can create real testimonials online in 24 hours & why it's important

These days if you want to sell anything to customers who don't know you and it's their first time to buy something from you they will look for anything which may convince them to trust you , they look at your social media pages likes, followers,

But they will also look for other people's comments about your business, however they do not believe anything simply written on your website , so to solve that problem you have to integrate facebook comments to your website, people will trust it more,

 Small Business Marketing

Here is how to create a facebook comment box :

With the recent introduction of Facebook's new and improved social plugin Comments Box, third party websites can not only add Facebook comments to their website, but they also have the option to sync comments directly to user Facebook pages. While in the past, the Comments Box served merely as a static addition to third party sites, it now has the capacity to provide direct communication between a website, a Facebook user, and all of his or her friends.

Using the new Comments Box, if you were to comment on a website such as www.dma4u.co.uk , you would be given the option to post both to www.dma4u.co.uk as well as to your Facebook wall and the newsfeeds of all of your friends via the checkbox seen above. In addition, if a friend of yours were to comment on your wall post, that comment would also appear on www.dma4u.co.uk What's more is that not only can you comment on third party sites using your personal Facebook username, but you can also leave comments under the name of a Facebook Page.

Also included in the new Comments box is a feature intended to increase quality of the plugin for users. Using social signals such as friends, friends of friends, and most liked or most active discussion threads, the Comments box will personalize results for each user.

How to add the Facebook Comments Box to my website

Facebook offers a simple and easy to use **Comments Box code generator** http://developers.facebook.com/docs/reference/plugins/comments/

which looks something like this:

Insert the URL you want Facebook to link to, the number of posts you would like displayed be default, and the width you want your Comments Box to be, then click "Get Code."

Or, add the Facebook Comments Box using the following code:

<div id="fb-root"></div><script src="http://connect.facebook.net/en_US/all.js#appId=APP_ID&xfbml=1"></script><fb:comments href="YOUR URL HERE" num_posts="10" width="500"></fb:comments>

Attributes

Href – the URL for the specific Comments plugin. Newsfeed stories on Facebook will link here.

Width – the width of the plucin in pixels (minimum width: 350px)

Num_posts – the number of comments to show by default

Moderation

Before adding admins to your comment box, you must first locate the ID of the user you wish to add. To do so, hover over a link to the user's name on Facebook, and a URL will appear in the lower left hand corner of your browser. Toward the end of the URL, you will find "id=" followed by a set of numbers. Those numbers make up the user ID.

Now that you have found your ID, you can add admins to your Comments Box by inputting the user IDs of each admin, separated by commas, into the following tag:

<meta property="fb:admins" content="{USER 1, USER 2, etc.}"/>

You can also associate a Facebook app with your Comments Box, automatically making all admins of the app admins of your Comments Box as well. Do so using the following tag:

<meta property="fb:app_id" content="{YOUR ID HERE}"/>

If you need help doing this visit www.dma4u.co.uk and ask for help

 Small Business Marketing

#44 How & what promotional gifts will keep small businesses in customers mind for a very long time

You should give away some promotional gifts to your customers to make them keep you in mind, but what promotional gifts are the best and will remain longer with your customers is the question,

Think about anything related to your business which doesn't cost much and think of attaching your business details on it and give it away to your customers

Some businesses may not find anything related to their business to give away, and then you should go for stationeries you can buy them at a very good price,

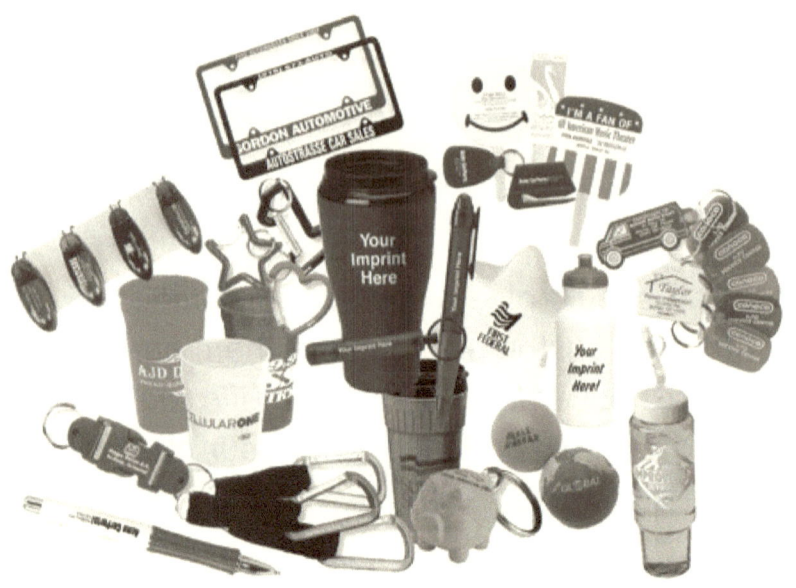

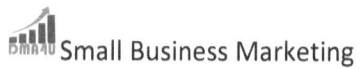 Small Business Marketing

#45 Where to get amazing promotional gifts for as cheap as $0.05 with free shipping worldwide

If you want to surprise your customers with gifts others don't give away because they think it expensive,

It's because they don't know where they can buy those for unbelievable prices,

Buy it from where they have been produced, guess where that can be? China and the easiest way to buy these is from alibaba.com you can order directly from Chinese manufacturers and they will post it to your door step wherever you are.

If you want to be different you must do different things and think out of the box.

Go on alibaba.com website look at all those products there and you will be surprised.

 Small Business Marketing

#46 How writing a blog can help small businesses to get found in Google

Start writing a blog, say something about your everyday job or anything which is related to your business,

Give advice on products or services related to your business, and link whatever you write to your website, try to mention keywords related to your business in your writings

Blog is one the most important ways to give credit to your website to get higher ranking in search engines

Below are some places you create a blog for free

 Small Business Marketing

Blogger

www.Wordpress.com

www.posterous.com

 Small Business Marketing

#47 Why small businesses should send a thank you letter & how it makes customers loyal to you

Don't let your customers to forget about you because if they do, someone else will do their job next times not you. Your biggest assets are your current customers so try to keep them .

They may not physically keep that thank you letter but they will be happy that even after you have been paid you still think and care about them, they will keep that in mind and it will psychologically affect them to be loyal to your business

 Small Business Marketing

 Small Business Marketing

#48 How Google remarketing will keep showing your ad to people who visited your website once

You may have already experienced going to a website or trying to buy some product and you just left that website without buying anything however suddenly you keep seeing that product or business's ads on other websites you, it's not a miracle or an accident, it happens through Google remarketing, the website you visited first has installed a cookie on it which is given to it by Google, then that cookie stores your details , and whenever you

 Small Business Marketing

visit any of Google partner sites they will show you ads related to the website you visited first.

This is an amazing feature which will help you to keep being in front of those who had a little interest in your product or service but they haven't been convinced or still didn't make decision to place order, and this ad will keep reminding them about your product or service.

you pay per click for it so if they never visit your website again even after seeing those ads you pay nothing and you didn't lose anything , but if they return then there must be a reason and its more likely they place an order

if you need help installing Google remarketing on your website visit www.dma4u.co.uk

 Small Business Marketing

#49 What are other low cost places on the internet for small businesses to advertise?

There are several more places you can advertise your business online, which are not very popular yet, however as long as they can get you to your target market and send you visitors, you shouldn't mind trying them.

And keep this in mind if they are less popular they will cost you less, for example google since its very popular it may cost more than any other pay per click advertising on the internet however that doesn't mean you shouldn't advertise on others , search is search as long people search for you and you pay per click there is no difference

It's almost the same for other cases

Below are a few more places you can advertise online

 Small Business Marketing

1) 7 search   www. 7search.com

A smaller player in the paid search industry, 7 Search uses smaller, niche search engines to display your Pay Per Click (PPC) ads. They claim a better ROI than their bigger competitors and bidding on keywords is cheaper than both Google Adwords and Microsoft Ad Center.

2) Stumbleupon   Paid   Discovery
www.stumbleupon.com/pd/

Still relatively unknown to most people, Stumbleupon drives more website traffic than both Facebook and Twitter. Stumbleupon is a neat social service people use to discover (stumble on) new websites they never knew existed, related to their interests. It's simple to use, create a profile, select your interests and start stumbling! Stumbleupon has an advertising platform called Paid Discovery where you pay between .05 cents and .25 cents for every person that stumbles on your site. You can select the interests you want your website to be included in and pay according to how targeted you want your stumbles to be. There are no advertisements here, the website page you select becomes your ad for visitors. While I love Stumbleupon, I would only consider using it if you have a product or service that has general appeal as it's not nearly as targeted as PPC or Facebook advertising.

3) Twitter Advertising:
www.business.twitter.com/twitter-smaller-businesses

While Twitter has allowed advertising for quite some time with promoted tweets and trends, it has been way out of the budget for small business owners (unless you had a min of 10k to spend a day!). Recently, Twitter launched a small business advertising program that will make it much more affordable for businesses to advertise on Twitter. Currently it's invitation only via a partnership with American Express, but will be opening up to everyone shortly. Lot's of potential here for the right businesses

4) LinkedIn Ads
www.linkedin.com/advertising

If you're in the BtoB or professional services industry, LinkedIn Ads may be exactly what you're looking for. Linkedin can serve highly targeted ads to other professionals and businesses on Linkedin. The Cost Per Click (CPC) is higher than pretty much any other platform listed here (there is also a minimum daily spend), but you can target your ads to very specific people. I would recommend this if you are BtoB or offering professional services and you are looking to acquire high value clients.

 Small Business Marketing

If you need create a new campaign on any of these , visit www.dma4u.co.uk

 Small Business Marketing

#50 Where to get 20 minutes of free marketing consultation for small businesses

If you want to save time and get a professional help to grow your business contact DMA4U www.dma4u.co.uk wherever in the world you are we can do market research and create a professional marketing plan for your business, we take care of your business and you sit back relax and provide perfect customer services to your customers,

Readers of this book are eligible for 20 minutes free marketing consultation so act now its free what are you waiting for visit www.dma4u.co.uk

 Small Business Marketing

For more marketing and business related books published by DMA4U visit

www.dma4u.co.uk/marketing-books

www.ingramcontent.com/pod-product-compliance
Lightning Source LLC
Chambersburg PA
CBHW032014170526
45157CB00002B/694